BRIDGE, ZIA

...and me

MICHAEL ROSENBERG

BRIDGE, ZIA
ZIA
...and me

MASTER POINT PRESS
TORONTO

Master Point Press
22 Lower Village Gate
Toronto, Ontario Canada
M5P 3L7
(416) 932-9766
Internet www.pathcom.com/~raylee/

Distributed in the USA by Barricade Books
150 Fifth Avenue, Suite 700
New York, NY 10011
(800) 59-BOOKS

Distributed in the UK by Chess & Bridge Ltd.
369 Euston Road
London NW1 3AR
+44-171-3882404 or www.bridgemagazine.co.uk

Canadian Cataloguing in Publication Data
Rosenberg, Michael, 1954-
Bridge, Zia... and me

ISBN 1-894154-04-5

1. Rosenberg, Michael, 1954-   . 2. Mahmood, Zia. 3. Bridge players — United States — Biography. I. Title

GV1282.26.R67A3 1999   795.41'5'092   C98-932-696-9

| *Editor* | Karen McCallum |
| *Cover and Interior design* | Olena S. Sullivan |

Printed and bound in Canada
1 2 3 4 5 6 7   06 05 04 03 02 01 00 99

To Edgar Kaplan, who represented all that is good and fair in the game of bridge. Through his writing and our memory of his words, he lives on as the most positive influence ever to touch the game we love.

ACKNOWLEDGMENTS

Firstly, major thanks must go to my editor and proofreader, Karen McCallum. Thanks to her, I have advanced from computer illiterate to computer idiot.

Over the years, I had noticed that, whenever I discovered a mistake in analysis in *The Bridge World*, invariably, a few months later, there would be a letter from John H. Lindsey III pointing out said error (there were also letters pointing out errors that I had missed). Therefore, I conceived the idea of asking Mr. Lindsey to check the bridge analysis in this book, and he agreed to do so. Particular thanks to John Hathaway Lindsey III.

Special thanks to Zia, who was the inspiration for this book, and for everything that fascinates me about the game of bridge. He taught me so much about the game, and revealed its beauty to me.

I would like to thank all of my other bridge mentors (in temporal order) — Colin Weir, Brian Spears, Barnet Shenkin, Victor Silverstone, Tony Priday, Ira Rubin, Matthew Granovetter, Pamela Granovetter, Debbie Rosenberg and Michael Kamil. All of these people talked at length with me about the game and added to my knowledge at various times during my playing career. Also, thanks to Edgar Kaplan, whose writings were the source of my knowledge regarding ethics in bridge.

I have tried to thank those responsible for contributing hands as they come up in the book. I am unclear as to the true origin of some of the hands. For example, after I had completed this book, but before it was published, I read Ottlik and Kelsey's *Adventures in Card Play* for the first time. I noticed three or four hands that had the same theme as hands in the 'My Favorite Hands' chapter. But I had learned these hands from different sources in the mid-70's, while that book was not published till the early 80's. I only feel a little guilty since, when I wrote my book, I was not aware that these hands had already appeared in a book. As to the authenticity of all the hands in the book, I have endeavored to be completely truthful. If I write that I witnessed something which happened, then I did. If I write that someone told me something happened, then that is all I know about it.

I apologize to anyone whom I accidentally failed to thank.

Finally, I would like to thank Debbie, who put up with me during all the time it took me to complete this book.

Michael Rosenberg

FOREWORD

As you read this book, you will find, as I have discovered through some twenty-five years of friendship, that Michael has the most fascinating mind for bridge you will ever encounter.

It is a well known 'secret' in the expert community that, if Rosenberg can't solve it, the problem is too difficult! So it is fair to warn you that this is not a book for the casual reader. I advise you to fasten your seat belt, for the journey will not be short — but it will be rewarding.

The scope will range enormously — he might introduce you to an innocuous-looking combination such as:

Dummy
♠ 10 5

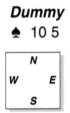

Declarer
♠ K Q

How would you play 3NT on the lead of a spade? (Play the ten to confuse West as to the location of the nine.)

Or he might be showing you one of his fifteen 'gems' — frustratingly ingenious hands, many of which will give you sleepless nights. Some are so difficult that, even after reading the answer, I defy you to return to the book a week later and solve them!

As you read his story, you will soon relate to the author's infectious love for the game. His views on ethics are frank and outspoken — but he makes no excuses for dealing in detail with this often-neglected subject, for it is very dear to his heart.

All those who aspire to the top will not be able to do without this book, but it will provide the most pleasure for those who, like me, are happily addicted to the passion that is bridge.

Anyone can win a world championship! At the expert level today, the competition has become so fierce that there is little to choose between the top players and teams. (Just look at the results of the last ten years.) This truth makes it all the more amazing that, at the 1998 World Championships in Lille, there was one player with so great a reputation that it would have created a bigger stir if he had *not* won the gold medal, than he actually did by winning.

That player was, of course, Michael Rosenberg. That event was the World Par Contest, easily the most challenging event devised to date.

But, the label, 'greatest technician of the game' has a sterile sound, which does injustice to the versatility of his great talent.

Zia

CONTENTS

AN
OPENING
WORD

These are my ramblings about me and bridge: what I find fascinating, what I find funny, and what I want to say. I hope you enjoy reading about my thoughts and experiences as much as I enjoyed reminiscing about them.

The author during play in the 1976 Sunday Times *Pairs event, with partner Barnet Shenkin. The opponents are Leon Tintner (France) and Leon Yallouze (Egypt).*

CHAPTER ONE

MEETING ZIA

London, 1975

"Five spades."

"Double."

"Redouble!"

I was drawn by what Jack London (had he been a bridge player) would have named 'the call of the slam.' True, five spades redoubled was not a slam, but in some ways it was better, so I walked over to the table to see what was happening. The first thing I observed was a good-looking, dark-skinned young man — there was something unusually flamboyant about him.

The diamond ten had been led. Dummy was tabled, and this is what I (and he) saw:

Dummy

♠ 10 7 4 2
♥ A 9 6 3
♦ 5 4
♣ A 5 3

Flamboyant Declarer

♠ A K Q J 5
♥ 5 4
♦ K Q J 7 2
♣ 6

East won the ♦A and returned the three. Without pausing for a nanosecond, our hero inserted the seven. West ruffed, but the hand was over. I was amazed, not only by the play (he had played East to have made the error of not returning a higher diamond) but also by the speed of execution. Of course, I realized that the bidding (which I never discovered) may have made the play obvious, but even so I was impressed.

"Who is that?" I asked Steve, the club manager.

"Who? Oh, him — that's Marmalade."

"Who?" I persisted.

"Mar... er... Zia Mahmood. He's from Pakistan. He's weird, but he can make some good plays."

That evening, I played my first rubber with Zia. On the first hand I held, as dealer:

♠ A   ♥ 10 x x x   ♦ 10 x x x   ♣ Q x x x

I passed, LHO passed, and Zia opened 3♣. RHO doubled and I, in my innocence, bid 5♣. After two passes RHO doubled again, which concluded the bidding. As was customary, declarer and dummy exchanged hands — Zia had a big smile all over his face. I looked at his hand and saw a blur of small cards, not more than four of which were clubs! The shock prevented me from determining his exact hand — we were playing for money! Meanwhile the club king had been led, and Zia inspected the dummy studiously. After a moment, he announced, "I'll settle for one down." There was no reaction. "All right, two down." The opponents were wavering. "Okay, three down, but that's my last offer." They threw their cards in and took +500.

My bridge 'education' had begun.

My classroom was Stefan's Bridge Club, which was situated near Marble Arch in London (the club has since closed down). I got the most important part of my bridge training there, in one cramped, crowded, smoke-filled room, at the top of a narrow flight of stairs. For a little over eighteen months I played there almost every day from 2:00 p.m. until midnight, and frequently later. The only exceptions I can remember are the trips I took to play bridge in Philadelphia, Vittel, New York, Juan-les-Pins and Copenhagen; the week-long trip to Rome that I won in a bridge tournament; and the day I went to see Hampton Court Palace (with Zia). I lived, ate, drank and slept bridge, and Stefan's was the perfect setting for me.

When I first came to London, I was living in the house of my friend Victor Silverstone. Victor had been part of Scotland's strongest partnership (with Willie Coyle), until he moved to London. His house was in Bushy Heath, about ten miles outside of London, and I stayed there with Victor, his wife, Linda, and their four young children. They showed me great hospitality and made my life very easy. I would come back in the early hours of the morning, or sometimes not at all, but they never demurred, even though it must have been somewhat disruptive having me there. Eventually, I rented a flat close to the bridge club.

CHANGING THE RULES

Zia was my teacher — although he wasn't aware of it. To be sure, I taught him some things too, about technical aspects of card-play, but I soon learned that technique was relatively unimportant in the long run. Who you were playing against was at least as important as what cards they played. What mattered was making unmakable contracts and breaking unbreakable ones. Zia didn't play by what I had thought of as the 'rules.' Take for example the following layout:

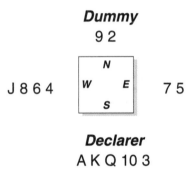

Dummy

9 2

J 8 6 4   7 5

Declarer

A K Q 10 3

The 'rules' state that declarer makes four tricks and the defense one; but if Zia knew (or even thought) that West had length, he would unhesitatingly lead small from hand. Of course, this meant that he would occasionally go down in a cold contract (East having Jx), but it was simply a matter of probability. A side advantage of this philosophy was that it was difficult to play and defend hands against him, since you couldn't rely on him playing a 'normal' card.

Here is another instructive situation which showed the

change in my thinking:

Dummy
10 5

```
      N
  W       E
      S
```

Declarer
A K Q 6

B.Z.* (presuming that a 6-1 break is precluded by the bidding, so that stiff jack is not a consideration), I would have thought that the best chance for four tricks lay in finding West with precisely 987; but now it was a question of whether to lead small to the ten, or to hope that the ten wasn't covered. This might hinge more upon whom I was playing against than anything else.

NOT THE BEST

Zia was not the only interesting player at Stefan's — in fact, thinking back, most of the regulars seemed like characters out of Victor Mollo's menagerie. Before I had played at the club a week, I heard stories about one player (I'll call him 'Enzo'), whom Steve (the manager) had told me was clearly the worst player in the world. One story, which appears in Zia's book *Bridge My Way*, tells of how Enzo defended seven notrump doubled on lead with two aces and, of course, failed to defeat it. Another tale went as follows: Enzo held

♠ x x x   ♥ A K Q x x x x x   ♦ x x   ♣ —

The bidding proceeded: 1♥ to Enzo's left, double, 2♣.

* Before Zia

Enzo chose to pass, and his LHO bid 2♥. Partner doubled again and there the bidding rested. He led the heart ace which, as you have no doubt noticed, was a tad precipitate as it was not his lead. The club manager on duty was called to the table to give a ruling. When his amusement had subsided (upon discovering that Enzo was defending 2♥ doubled without ever having made a bid), he explained declarer's rights. Declarer then said to Enzo's partner, "Lead a trump." So he led a spade.

This was what Enzo saw:

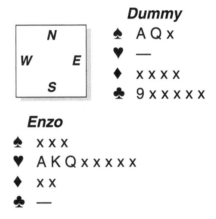

Dummy
♠ A Q x
♥ —
♦ x x x x
♣ 9 x x x x x

Enzo
♠ x x x
♥ A K Q x x x x x
♦ x x
♣ —

The opening spade lead ran to the jack, and declarer played the heart jack. Enzo, simultaneously giggling and counting on his fingers, ducked. Declarer now played the heart ten. After more giggling and counting, Enzo figured that declarer had to make another trick in this suit, so he ducked again! Declarer now cashed the ace-king of diamonds, finessed the queen of spades and cashed the ace before leading a third diamond from dummy. Declarer's full hand was:

♠ J x x   ♥ J 10 9 8 7   ♦ A K   ♣ K x x

2♥ doubled made!

Although I heard each of these stories from more than one source, I did not, *could not*, believe them. Would you?

♠ ♥ ♦ ♣

Soon afterwards, Enzo came into the club and I had the chance to observe him in action. This was an early hand:

Dummy
♠ x x
♥ x x
♦ K J x
♣ A K Q x x x

Enzo
♠ Q x x
♥ K Q x x
♦ x x x x
♣ x x

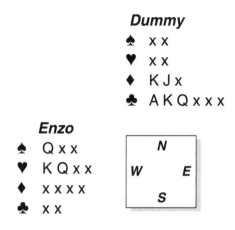

I don't remember the bidding, but the contract was 4♠ after declarer had bid both majors. Enzo led a diamond, and the trick continued king, ace, small. His partner returned the ace and a small heart. Enzo won and shifted to... yes, you guessed it — a trump! Declarer held:

♠ A K J x x ♥ J 10 x x x ♦ x ♣ J x,

and now made the hand. I began to wonder if those stories were indeed true.

I remember once cutting Enzo and picking up a twenty-count. Thoughtlessly, I said, 'Stop, 2NT.' ('Stop' is the British equivalent of 'Skip-bid, please wait.') Of course, Enzo passed with his seven-count. The sight of dummy evoked a smile from my LHO, British international Robert Sheehan — the only time I can recall him showing any emotion at the table.

Another amazing, authentic, Enzo debacle:

Dummy

♠ 9 x
♥ x x
♦ A J 9
♣ K J 10 x x x

Enzo

♠ A x x x
♥ A K Q x x
♦ K 4
♣ x x

Zia	?	Me	Enzo
WEST	NORTH	EAST	SOUTH
			1♥
pass	2♣	pass	2NT
pass	3♣	pass	3NT
dbl	pass	pass	redbl
all pass			

Zia led a spade to my jack, which our hero ducked. I played the spade queen which Enzo ducked. Zia overtook with the king and continued with the spade ten, which was ducked (!) — dummy and I both pitched hearts. Zia, figuring that Enzo couldn't duck many more spades, shifted to the three of diamonds. Enzo studied this with great intensity, and the longer he thought, and the more he perspired, the clearer it became that it was vital to his well-being to guess from which diamond Zia had led away. Finally, he played the nine, and when I produced the ten he was so agitated that he won the king and immediately shot back the four. This was the full deal:

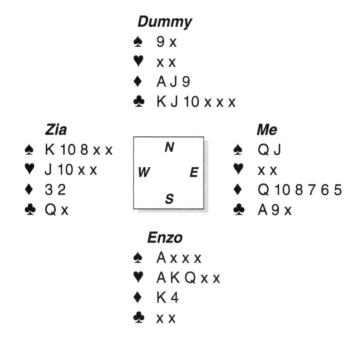

Dummy
- ♠ 9 x
- ♥ x x
- ♦ A J 9
- ♣ K J 10 x x x

Zia
- ♠ K 10 8 x x
- ♥ J 10 x x
- ♦ 3 2
- ♣ Q x

Me
- ♠ Q J
- ♥ x x
- ♦ Q 10 8 7 6 5
- ♣ A 9 x

Enzo
- ♠ A x x x
- ♥ A K Q x x
- ♦ K 4
- ♣ x x

I won the queen and cleared diamonds. Enzo now completed the debacle by trying the club king, so the final tally was -2800. Not bad for a hand which, on normal play, would produce +1350 or +1750. Zia had doubled because, in his thinking, he needed a reason *not* to double Enzo.

The proof of the pudding is in the eating.

If you play enough rubber bridge, you'll see almost everything. I remember being on lead against the simple auction 1NT-4♠. I led my singleton club trying for a ruff, and got it *at trick one*. Another hand I heard about (but did not see) produced a result of three notrump doubled making with two overtricks, with 150 honors against.

(Think about it.)

THE STYLE

Through Zia, I developed a 'style' of dummy play in which the *ability to make the contract* was considered to be the most pertinent factor. Thus, we would prefer to play a slam which required guessing a queen to one which had a 65% chance of success.

We hated to commit ourselves early in the hand — even when it was clearly correct to do so. For example, if the opponents led a suit in which dummy had KJxx and we had Ax, we would never play the jack at trick one, even though there are many hands where it is 'necessary' as a discovery play. Our thinking was that we would 'find' the queen anyway after playing low, either from RHO's behavior at trick one, or through other information gained later in the hand. (This is one example of something we later had to adjust when playing against 'real' players.)

Another aspect of 'The Style' concerned drawing trumps. Most educators teach that you should draw trumps unless you have a good reason not to do so. Zia and I had the opposite philosophy. We preferred not to touch trumps until we could control the hand regardless of how they broke. (This applied more stringently to partscore deals.) Even today, when the right play is obviously to draw trumps, it takes me a few extra seconds to drag the card out of my hand.

Traditional wisdom says that notrump contracts are a race to establish tricks. You play your best suit, and they play theirs. Zia wisdom differed: if he sometimes played *their* best suit, maybe they would attack *his* best suit. I have witnessed this strategy succeed many times, even when it should have been obvious to the defenders. An example of this in action can be seen later in this book. Here is an illustrative hand which I invented:

Dummy
- ♠ K J 10 6
- ♥ 7 5 2
- ♦ J 10 8
- ♣ 7 5 2

Declarer
- ♠ A Q 4
- ♥ K Q J 9
- ♦ 7 5 2
- ♣ J 10 8

You open a weak notrump and play it there. West leads a spade and you win the jack in dummy. Most people would play a heart now, but you know that they will likely win the first or second round and cash their minors. At match-points, you might try to sneak one heart through and run with five tricks, but at IMPs or rubber bridge you would rather try to make the hand. Win the spade in dummy and play a club toward the jack. This might succeed in either of two ways. Firstly, East may rise and shift to a heart, and if West has the ace you will probably make one notrump. Secondly, if West wins the club, a heart shift from, say, ♥10xx, may look the most attractive from his viewpoint — and again you may well make the contract.

Note that despite the fact that you have equal combined holdings in the minors, it is clear to attack clubs; dummy's diamond holding can act as a deterrent. You should also note that it is remotely possible that the club jack will win the trick, West ducking the ace and East playing low with the king-queen. Probably your best shot now is a diamond, creating total confusion. Strangely, West may now defeat a hand that might have made had he won the club!

Playing with a weak partner against Zia one afternoon at Stefan's, I recall a hand which had a unique feature. I, vulnerable against not, held:

♠ Q x x x   ♥ K J x x x   ♦ J   ♣ J x x

He and my partner passed, and RHO opened 1♣. I passed, Zia responded 1♦, partner bid 1♥ and RHO cuebid 2♥. I began to ponder the best tactical bid. After about ten seconds had elapsed, Zia turned impatiently toward me and said, "It makes no difference."

"What do you mean?" I asked, confused.

"Just do something," he said.

I bid 4♥. He bid 4NT, followed by 6♦ which was cold. (The Anti-Key-Card-Blackwood faction will be pleased to know that he was missing an ace and the trump king, but this did not discomfit him since the trump suit was A1098xxx facing Qxxx.) He had been thinking that he was bidding slam, and that I was never going to prolong the rubber by sacrificing; so what I did was irrelevant (he was right). Sure, people have told their opponents that "it makes no difference" before, but not *during the bidding*.

THE DOCTOR IS IN

Another memorable character at Stefan's was the late Dr. Alan Manch. Besides being a good player, he had a constant stream of dry wit which I found entertaining. He would call Zia 'twisted and perverted', but I think he secretly held a great respect for him.

The doctor once showed me the following suit-combination:

Dummy

J 8 7 5

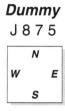

Declarer

A Q 9 6

"How do you play for three tricks?" he inquired.

"I know this one," I answered. "Most people cash the ace and try to guess who has king-ten fourth, but the right play is small to the queen, followed by cashing the ace if it loses. This pays off only to a bare king with West."

"Correct. And what if you are in your hand with only one entry to dummy?"

I took a few seconds and said, "The ace is still wrong. I lead the queen, and subsequently play so that I lose only to a bare king in either hand."

"You're too good," he said, slightly crestfallen.

I comforted him with, "It's a really nice combination. I'm glad you taught it to me."

Notice, however, that in the latter case, when playing against opponents who always play the deuce when they hold the three or the four or both (and always play the three when holding the four), playing the ace is as good as the queen, since only when opponents play the three and the deuce do you have a guess.

In fact, most suit-combinations should not be played in a vacuum — the opponents are part of the problem.

Suit-combinations fascinated me, and continue to do so. My favorite back then was:

Dummy
Q 10 8 7 6

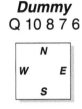

Declarer
A 5

Looking for four tricks, you play the ace and everyone follows small — what now? It's exactly even, you say. Why are you wasting my time? I'll come back to that.

Now suppose that, when you play the ace, it goes small, small, *nine*. Small to the queen becomes the 'percentage' play since it gains against J9 and J9x, and loses only to K9x. But wait a minute! This means that a smart RHO will play the nine from K9x, but not from J9x. So maybe the 'right' play is small to the ten. And going back to the original proposition, what can be inferred from RHO's *failure* to play the nine? Perhaps the queen is now the percentage guess. And what if it goes ace, small, small, *jack*? Is that king-jack doubleton? Jack-nine doubleton? J9x?

There were some terrible players at Stefan's, but we did have some really strong games. When the table consisted of any four of Zia, myself, Sam Lev, Irving Rose, Rob Sheehan and Martin Hoffman, I found the game even more exciting than usual. As it happened, I was extremely successful in strong games (I randomly held good cards). I learned through Zia not to complain about bad luck. Instead, when I lost, I would focus on my own shortcomings. The only time I can recall Zia complaining was this: after I had won eight consecutive rubbers in a strong game, I cut Manch and said, "C'mon, Doctor. It's your turn to win a rubber."

"It's your turn to lose one, you mean," said Zia with a glare. (I won the rubber.)

Two other interesting characters at Stefan's were Sam Lev and Martin Hoffman. Both were undisciplined bidders (a plus at Stefan's, where defenses were rarely top-notch), brilliant card-players, lightning analysts (mostly accurate) and complete result merchants. They were both hard on their partners, and had great table presence.

I remember I sometimes baited Martin when I watched or played at his table. During a hand, I would silently analyze the play of some contract other than the one that was being declared. Then, after the hand, I would make a comment such as, "Your side could have made two spades," or, "You can defeat four clubs." I didn't care that the contract had actually been three notrump or four hearts. I had seen something fascinating or tricky, and I taunted Martin with it. He would invariably argue but, no matter how good he was, he couldn't out-analyze me when I had had time to think about a position and he had not.

In bidding, Zia and I were notably different. By nature, he was an overbidder, and I an underbidder. Despite this contrast, one similarity which we shared was the childlike thrill we got out of bidding small slams. Perhaps that's why I adopted his phony cuebid weapon as part of my arsenal. The purpose of a fake cuebid or trial bid was to prevent that lead against a game or slam. Rubber bridge was the perfect setting for this, since partner generally had no more idea than the opponents of what was going on, and therefore nothing untoward was taking place (not that we knew anything about ethics in those days). As some of the smarter players caught on, you could mix it up a bit and cuebid the suit you actually *wanted* led.

Of course, this strategy could easily backfire, and Zia (or I) would be left looking silly. But it was a fundamental law of 'The Style' that we did not care how we looked. How many times have you said, or heard another player say, "I felt he had that, but I couldn't play for it because it was too much against the odds"? Why not? How else can you ever test the validity of your 'feelings'?

Zia was also more flamboyant on opening lead than I but, although my initial reaction was scornful, I eventually came to realize that there could be justification for 'flashy' leads. I once held, as West:

♠ A J 5 3 ♥ K 10 7 4 2 ♦ Q 7 2 ♣ 5

The bidding was:

NORTH	SOUTH
	1♠
2♣	3♠
4♦	4♥
4♠	pass

As early as North's 4♦ bid, I started planning my defense.

Clearly, I had two trump tricks, but it would be nice if I could score a third trump by ruffing a club. I could lead a club and try to find partner's entry after winning the spade ace. That entry could not be in diamonds, not only because partner didn't double 4♦, but also because, with the opponents trying for slam, there was no room for him to hold a king. No, it would have to be the heart queen. But if I led a club, won the spade ace, and shifted to the heart king, declarer might see what was happening and duck. This was the full deal:

Dummy
♠ 9 6
♥ J 9 5 3
♦ A K 5
♣ A J 8 6

Me
♠ A J 5 3
♥ K 10 7 4 2
♦ Q 7 2
♣ 5

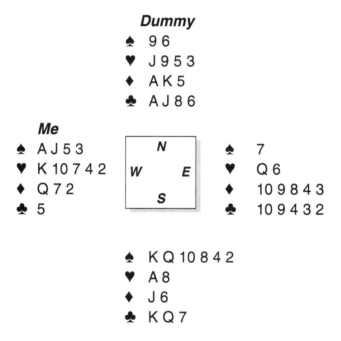

♠ 7
♥ Q 6
♦ 10 9 8 4 3
♣ 10 9 4 3 2

♠ K Q 10 8 4 2
♥ A 8
♦ J 6
♣ K Q 7

I led the heart *king*. Declarer won, crossed to a diamond, and played a spade. I won, shifted to a club, and set the game. (Declarer could have made the hand by ducking the heart at trick one, but who would do that?) B.Z., such a lead would not have even occurred to me.

At that time in my career, I had no trepidation in playing my feelings: that was one of my strengths. But, despite all I had learned from Zia, I was more aware than ever of how much more there was to discover.

CHAPTER TWO

EARLY DAYS

Glasgow, 1970

What about life before Stefan's?

I don't remember exactly how I learned bridge — there were two introductions. In 1970, when I was sixteen, my father signed up for bridge lessons and bought a bridge book for beginners. He dropped out after a couple of lessons and never read the book. I found the book and read it. At about the same time my high school started a bridge club which I joined.

I had been playing chess seriously, but was becoming frustrated over my lack of improvement. I had represented Scotland in the Students' (under-27) Team Olympiads in East Germany (1969) and Israel (1970), and was soon to compete in the (individual) World Junior Chess Championships in Greece. Having shown great promise earlier (I had beaten the Scottish Champion at age thirteen), I felt I was stagnating. I welcomed the chance to explore a new game.

Soon after I started playing, someone (sorry, I don't remember who) gave me a copy of *Bridge in the Menagerie* by Victor Mollo. I stayed up all night reading it. Aside from loving the characterizations, I found the bridge positions so exciting and so beautiful that I was 'gone' on bridge forever. It is still one of my favorite books — I can recite many passages from it, and other *Menagerie* books. One of my 'Hog' favorites goes something like this:

> *"What a way to present a problem,"* snorted the Hideous Hog, disgustedly crumpling up someone's newspaper. *"South to make four spades against best defense! What sort of South, I ask you, allows East-West to put up the best defense?"*
>
> *"But..."* began Oscar the Owl.
>
> *"Nonsense,"* interrupted the Hog. *"If East-West put up the best defense, it can only mean that South doesn't know his business. So why should anyone care how this ignoramus sets about taking ten tricks?"*

I played a lot of bridge hands in those early days, some of them by myself. I also played all-night sessions at the weekend with Brian Spears (my best friend), Jack Silverstone and others. Both Brian and Jack represented Scotland, after I had emigrated to America. I once played thirty-six hours straight, and then slept for twenty-one hours — all a part of my (bridge) education.

VARSITY DAYS

In 1971, I went to Glasgow University, purportedly to study Law. Unfortunately (?), I found the Bridge Room and practically lived in it. I met my first serious mentor there — Colin Weir. Colin also seemed to reside in the Bridge Room. He was on the fringe of the Scottish team, and I believe he did play for Scotland at some point. He taught me a lot, none of which I can specifically now remember. Maybe I would disagree now with much of what he said, but maybe not. I remember him as being sensible and unopinionated. (This set him aside from most of Scotland's other top players.)

While I was learning the game and trying to put my 'advanced' theoretical knowledge into practice, I had the occasional 'accident.' I remember once, after I had been playing in the Bridge Room for several months, I was defending three notrump and partner led a heart. Declarer (Doug somebody) won the lead, and I could not tell if our hearts were running. Doug now led the jack of spades towards dummy's ♠AK109xx and ran it. I, with ♠Qx, ducked smoothly. Doug heaved a sigh of relief, played a spade to the ace and ended up making overtricks. Of course, we had four cashing heart tricks. While he was running the spades the following conversation took place.

PARTNER: Nice duck, partner. You should give up bridge.
ME: (to Doug) How could you play a spade to the ace?
DOUG: It was 100%.
ME: What are you talking about? Why couldn't I have a singleton, and my partner have queen to four (queen-fourth to Americans)?
DOUG: There are only thirteen spades in the deck.
ME: You had two spades, dummy had six, I could have had one...
DOUG: Dummy had *seven*!
ME: (Fierce blush)

My partner in this misadventure was Gerald Haase, with whom I formed my first serious partnership. He and I were selected to compete in the Scottish Trials (either 1972 or 1973 — I don't remember which), amidst considerable concern that we weren't ready. (I was nineteen, and had been playing for less than three years.) We finished second, silencing our critics, and went on to represent Scotland in the Camrose trophy, the annual tournament between Scotland, England, Wales and Northern Ireland. We played against Northern Ireland (we won) and England (we tied).

I recall one of our hands from the Rayne Cup (a Scottish team event), reported by ex-international Albert Benjamin, where he called me brilliant. I held as West:

$$\spadesuit \text{ A x x} \quad \heartsuit \text{ x x x} \quad \diamondsuit \text{ x x x x} \quad \clubsuit \text{ x x x}$$

The bidding, by one of Scotland's best pairs, playing Precision:

NORTH	SOUTH
	1♣[1]
2♣[2]	3♣[3]
3♠[4]	4♠[5]
5♣[6]	6♣
pass	

1. 16+ hcp.
2. 5+ clubs, 8+ HCP.
3. Asking in clubs.
4. Five-card clubs headed by two of top three honors.
5. Asking in spades.
6. Second-round control.

I couldn't have scripted it better — I led a low spade; Haase smartly held the queen over the ♠KJ, and the contract went one down. Of course, there was nothing 'brilliant' about it; in fact, it was pathetically obvious. If I had known the term then, I would have described this hand as a 'gimme.'

I recall giving Benjamin a hand for the newspaper. This was the crucial suit:

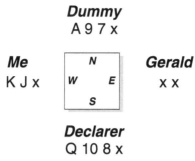

Dummy
A 9 7 x

Me
K J x

Gerald
x x

Declarer
Q 10 8 x

I was West, playing with Gerald in the Junior Camrose tournament, and this was the trump suit. Declarer led a plain suit from dummy and ruffed with the ten; I over-ruffed with the *king*. Subsequently, declarer cashed the ace and finessed the eight. The contract was 4♣ and this held declarer to ten tricks, but when I gave Benjamin the hand I told him the contract was *five* clubs, and that my defense had defeated it. A little while after the article was printed I ran into Benjamin, who looked somewhat upset.

"You did a terrible thing," he said.

"What do you mean?" I asked, knowing full well, and feeling as guilty as sin.

"That five clubs contract you defeated," he said. "Look!" And he showed me a letter.

"Dear Mr. Benjamin," it ran, "I refer to your column of... I have no doubt that you think this is very amusing, but I do not. To overruff with the king when you hold the jack (with the queen as yet unplayed) is one of the most unethical plays I have ever seen. That you should reward this player with an accolade instead of recommending his suspension, is shocking. Yours, etc." Ah well, you can't please everybody.

It was about this time that I read about the Grosvenor Gambit. The idea struck me as amusing, and I looked for opportunities to employ this apparently pointless strategy at the table. I was playing with Gerald in a Scottish Cup match against a team that included Hugh Kelsey and Tom Culbertson. Culbertson was declaring three notrump, and his diamonds were ♦Q10x in hand facing ♦A98x in dummy. He ran the queen, losing to my king. Before he attacked the suit again, I discarded a diamond. Then he ran the ten losing to my now singleton jack. When he discovered what I had done, he muttered something about 'kids these days.'

A few hands later, Culbertson was declaring 5♠. I won Gerald's lead and shifted to the heart ten into dummy's ♥AKxxx. Tom, who had started with ♥Jxxx, thought about this and played low, winning in dummy. He now eliminated the minors and threw partner in. Gerald exited with the ♥9. Tom knew that Gerald, holding ♥Q9x could have beaten the hand simply by giving a ruff-and-discard, but the earlier Grosvenor was preying on his mind. Had I really shifted to a heart from Q10 doubleton? After muttering some more about what these kids were doing to him, he went up and dropped my queen, spoiling the story. A pity.

My next partnership was with Barnet Shenkin, a young Glasgow player with whom I played fairly successfully for about five years, until I moved to the U.S. in 1978. Our most notable successes were the *Sunday Times* Pairs and the Gold Cup (a Knockout Teams event roughly equivalent to the Spingold in prestige). We played for Scotland in the Camrose Trophy on numerous occasions, and won it at least twice. The first time I played for Britain I was 21 years old; Barnet and I represented Great Britain in the Common Market Championships in Vittel in 1975 when we finished third. We also played for Britain in the European Championships in Copenhagen in 1977.

And now an opening lead problem. You hold as West:

♠ Q 10 6 4   ♥ 10 7 5 3   ♦ 4 2   ♣ 8 6 3

The bidding:

WEST	NORTH	EAST	SOUTH
	1♣	2♦	2♥
pass	3♦	pass	3♥
pass	4♣	pass	4♦
pass	4♠	pass	4NT
pass	5♠[1]	pass	5NT
pass	7♣	pass	7♥
pass	7NT	all pass	

1. Two key cards plus the heart queen.

It looks as if West has solid clubs, and East very good hearts plus the diamond ace. It might well be necessary to attack declarer's entry before he can unblock the (you hope) stiff queen of hearts. So you lead a diamond. At least it's partner's suit. The full deal:

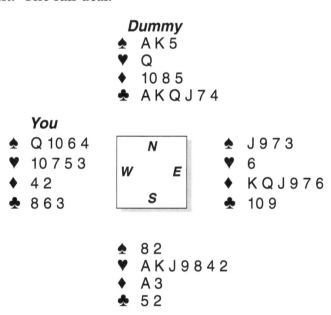

Dummy
♠ A K 5
♥ Q
♦ 10 8 5
♣ A K Q J 7 4

You
♠ Q 10 6 4
♥ 10 7 5 3
♦ 4 2
♣ 8 6 3

♠ J 9 7 3
♥ 6
♦ K Q J 9 7 6
♣ 10 9

♠ 8 2
♥ A K J 9 8 4 2
♦ A 3
♣ 5 2

Declarer wins the diamond and runs clubs. You must make three discards, and therefore cannot control spades. Then after the run of the three top hearts, East will have made six discards, and therefore will need to throw all his diamonds to retain spades.

Hope you led the correct diamond!

I played a hand very much like this at the 1998 Summer Nationals in Chicago. West actually held ♦102, and led the ten: but since he had only three hearts it was irrelevant.

Why do I bring up this hand now? Because it reminded me of one that I defended almost twenty-five years before. Playing with Barnet in the Scottish Trials, I was on lead against some contract with four-two doubleton in partner's suit. Others in my situation led the four, and declarer, holding ace-three doubleton now made the hand on a simple squeeze against partner. I, however, led the deuce and defeated the contract.

Am I that good? Not really. Barnet and I had the agreement to lead low from a doubleton in partner's suit!

Our results did not suffer when I moved to London to play rubber bridge for a living — if anything, we were a stronger pair. Our partnership effectively ended when I left Britain.

I returned to Scotland in August, 1978 (after I had moved to America), to play for Britain in the European Junior Championships in Stirling, partnering Richard Benstead. Since Barnet was over the age limit, I played for Scotland with Richard in the Junior Camrose, which Scotland won. We went on to win the European Junior Championship too.

CHAPTER THREE

AMERICA

New York, 1978

In February of 1978, I moved to America, intending to survive by playing bridge and backgammon in the New York City clubs. Zia had not yet moved to New York, but had begun making sporadic invasions into the Chicago-style game at the Cavendish Club. It took both of us a while to acclimate to the American style of bidding and play. I was not accustomed to feeling uncomfortable at the table, but it was so different from Britain that instead of feeling I knew everything that was happening, as I had at Stefan's, I now felt that I knew next to nothing.

I also found that I did not enjoy discussing the game as

much as I had in the U.K.. This was not due to my unfamiliarity, but rather to the focus of the American players.

In Britain, when someone said, "I have a hand for you," it was invariably a hand to play or defend; but here, it was a hand to bid. The attention was all on bidding, and I was only interested in the play. I didn't know if card-play was more important, but I knew I wanted it to be. I felt that you could figure out the clearly correct play much of the time, but you could hardly ever be certain of the right bid.

THE BEAST

It wasn't until 1984 that I began to appreciate and understand bidding. Then I started to play regularly against Ira Rubin (a.k.a. 'The Beast'). Until then, I had inwardly felt some measure of scorn for players who believed that they always knew the right bid — and here was one of the most opinionated persons I had ever encountered. Yet, there was a nagging ring of truth that forced me to listen to him — that, and the fact that he talked a lot.

Of course, Ira's four-card major system evoked memories of Britain (although his style was as dissimilar from British as it could possibly be). I began playing his basic system in a few tournaments, partnering Matthew and Pamela Granovetter and, for the first time, I found that I enjoyed the bidding.

And... I became interested in the bidding.

THOUGHTS ON BIDDING

(Finally, I had some!)

What is the purpose of bidding? To arrive at the best contract, yes. But what is the best contract? The one that will produce the best result on average — in practice.

When the bidding is over, you should then be sorry about every piece of accurate information you have provided — only the opponents can benefit now. It's so much more difficult to defend with less information — or worse yet, with misleading information.

To this end, I was already aware of phony cuebids and game tries, and I knew about psychic bids, but it had never occurred to me that you could begin your constructive auctions with the intention of gaining an advantage in the play. A prime example of this is the decision about which minor to open with 4-4. Those players who always open with the same suit are adding an 'element of ease' to their opponents' leads and subsequent defense. By varying intelligently, you can make life more difficult for them without hurting yourself appreciably.

I have never disclosed to anyone, not even to Zia, all of my rules governing which minor I open, but the factors involved are: a) ability to handle the auction; b) position; c) vulnerability; d) lead-inhibiting; e) lead-directional; f) strength of the opposition; g) the other table(s).

I like to combine varying the minor-suit opening with rebidding notrump on balanced hands — even if it means bypassing four-card majors (partner can always check back). This idea is not part of Ira's methods, although his four-card major opening style almost precludes a balanced hand when opener rebids one-of-a-major. And, I don't do it with every hand — only those where my distribution or honor dispersion makes it feel right.

The benefit of this approach can plainly be seen in the auction

NORTH	SOUTH
1♣	1♦
1NT	3NT
pass	

In old standard, opener can have only four distributions:

3-3-3-4, 3-3-2-5, 3-2-3-5, or 2-3-3-5. Playing my way, there are *thirteen* possible distributions. Yes, the opponents know that dummy has no four-card major, but that is of far less importance than knowing *which* four-card major declarer has, or that he has none. This idea could even be extended to opening the three-card suit with 4-3. Zia has even opened 1♣ in third chair with five diamonds and three clubs!

Another advantage of this style is the negative inference which arises when partner rebids one of a major — you now know many hands that he *can't* have. True, the opponents have this information also, but I believe that is less important on this auction. On the 1NT (rebid) - 3NT auctions the hidden information hurts only the opponents.

Ira's system can pose unfamiliar problems for the opponents, in that he can open, or rather, he relishes opening 1♠ on ♠5432 (weaker holdings not permitted). The 'standard' five-card major structure is excellent for constructive auctions, but it frequently makes the defenders' lives pathetically easy.

Even a convention such as Stayman, which most players view as essential, seems to me to be of doubtful value on balanced hands. Most of the time you will not uncover a fit (especially when you only have one major), and when you do your result may not be superior. When you don't find a fit you have given the opposition information about your hand, and more importantly about your partner's — information which may be crucial. In addition, you have given them a chance to double — or not double — Stayman for the lead (admittedly, this double is so abused that it sometimes works to your advantage). Are you *sure* it's all worth the trouble?

On the first deal of the final of the 1992 World Olympiad in Salsamaggiore, Italy, I held:

♠ 10 x x　♥ K Q x x x　♦ K 10　♣ 10 x x

My partner, Seymon Deutsch, opened a 15-17 1NT. I decided to force to game, and our methods did not allow me to offer a choice of games — I could play 4♥ whenever he had three hearts or, with Stayman, whenever he had four. Most players would attempt to do one of these, but I couldn't imagine a more perfect set of circumstances in which to put my theory into practice. It looked so much like a nine-trick hand to me. I envisioned my RHO leading a heart from ♥J9xx into Seymon's ace-ten doubleton. Perhaps he would make three notrump, while the other room would transfer to hearts and go down in two notrump! Confidently I bid 3NT. This backfired horribly when partner held:

♠ A K x　♥ A x x x　♦ A x x x　♣ x x

Worse still, opening leader had ♣KQJxx. I guess I'm stubborn, because I would do the same again. Note that, if one of partner's diamonds had been a club, then three notrump would have been best. There were many hands he could have held that would have made me a hero — instead I was the goat.

HURTING THE 'BAD GUYS'

One area of the game where you can 'hurt' your opponents is with eccentric penalty doubles. A recurring situation is: the opponents reach three notrump with a long suit after your side has opened the bidding. It is pointless to double them when you know they are going down unless either a) you think they may stay there, or b) you can also penalize the runout. However, it makes a good deal of sense to double when you think they are *making* three notrump. If they stay, your result might not be much worse (if the contract is unusual), but if you scare them out you show a huge gain.

I also see a strange advantage in doubling trump contracts with poor intermediates. If I double LHO's 4♠ contract with ♠AQ10x, he may finesse and hold me to one trick. If I double with ♠AQxx, maybe he finesses into partner's stiff ten, loses control and three trump tricks. If I don't double, I do better with ♠AQ10x and worse with ♠AQxx. That's what I mean by 'hurting' your opponents.

Similarly, when the bidding goes 1♥-(3♦)-dbl-(pass), I feel more comfortable passing with Axx(x) than with A10x(x). (So I'm weird — what else is new?)

Yet another idea which has occurred to me is this: during a competitive auction, if I feel fairly certain that my side is eventually going to land in a particular contract, I give thought to getting there slowly (usually by passing as opposed to just blasting game). For example: the bidding goes three passes to you, and you open 1♠ at favorable vulnerability. Partner raises to 2♠ and RHO doubles. Now, instead of bidding 4♠, you *pass*. It is most unlikely that your opponents, both passed hands, can exchange information that will result in a successful five-level action. However, it is very possible that you will gain information by allowing your LHO to bid — information that may help you make 4♠. There are recurring opportunities for this tactic.

Having said all this, I cannot honestly say that I have a strong opinion that 'my way' is better. I only know that I like it. And even if I'm only breaking even, I prefer to exchange some bidding accuracy for improved results in card-play. The only reason I have to think that I am gaining something is my personal experience, and I find that biases built on people's personal experience are generally unreliable.

OPINIONS

Speaking of bias, I regard it as a major block to learning. All the great bidding theorists seem to me to have difficulty separating opinion from truth.

Some experts believe five-card major openings are the only way. Others think that four-card majors are clearly superior. Or take, for example, the controversy between proponents of sound and light opening bids. Each side will cite numerous examples where their style gains. They can't both be right, so whom should you believe? Personally, I prefer the sound style — which is consistent with my general philosophy, since light openings generally make it tougher for the opponents (and partner!) in the bidding, while sound ones make it harder for them in the play (since you are in the auction less when they declare). My experience (there it goes again) is that opening light on balanced hands vulnerable, or opening light 4-4-4-1 hands, is a losing proposition. Other light openings break about even.

The answer to the question, "Whom should one believe?" is *nobody*. It seems clear to me that more bad results are caused by partners not being on the same wavelength than by any inherent inferiority of system. Therefore, the most important thing to do is to agree with your partner about what hands *you* will open. What you actually decide is relatively unimportant.

MY PARTNER (ZIA)

In 1989, I decided that I needed to make some money playing bridge, so I went to Zia and asked him what he thought

I should do. He was happy to play with me in the Nationals, but he was certain that nobody was going to hire us unless we won something. With hopes of doing so, we played in the 1989 Reisinger on a team with Sam Lev, Mark Molson, and Chris Compton — and fortunately we won. Due to Zia and Molson, our team was 'poisoned', so we could not compete in the U.S. international team trials. But Zia and I had made our mark. We were hired immediately, and in the next four National knockouts we won one and lost in the final twice.

Our partnership had several problems. In the beginning I was rusty — I had played little competitive bridge between 1981 and 1989. Because Zia expected better from me, he frequently became frustrated. Since we were friends, and because we had always said whatever we wanted to one another in the days when we played money bridge, Zia made no effort to control his feelings. This did not bother me, but it probably gave the opposition confidence. We did not play frequently in tournaments together, and our system was a hodgepodge of different things we had discussed over the previous fourteen years. Eventually, we started writing things down, but it was a long time before we knew what we were doing. Our major problem was, and still is, that we try too hard for perfection. When we play with other partners, we are practical players; with each other, we try to cover too many possibilities.

For the first eighteen months I was low on confidence. Then I realized something which turned it around for me. I had been reading about, and watching, the best players in the country, and they *all* made numerous errors. I could win, not because of how well I played, but because of how badly *they* played! Even Zia, whom I regarded as the best player, was 'hopeless'. I felt much better. I wasn't scared anymore.

This hand is from the 1992 Cap Gemini tournament in Holland.

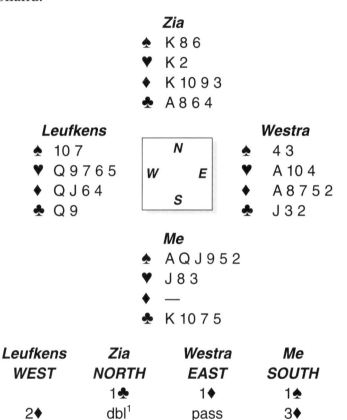

Zia
- ♠ K 8 6
- ♥ K 2
- ♦ K 10 9 3
- ♣ A 8 6 4

Leufkens
- ♠ 10 7
- ♥ Q 9 7 6 5
- ♦ Q J 6 4
- ♣ Q 9

Westra
- ♠ 4 3
- ♥ A 10 4
- ♦ A 8 7 5 2
- ♣ J 3 2

Me
- ♠ A Q J 9 5 2
- ♥ J 8 3
- ♦ —
- ♣ K 10 7 5

Leufkens WEST	Zia NORTH	Westra EAST	Me SOUTH
	1♣	1♦	1♠
2♦	dbl¹	pass	3♦
pass	3NT	pass	4♣
pass	4♠	all pass	

1. Support double

West led the diamond queen, covered and ruffed. The contract was in no real danger even if clubs were 4-1 since I could play loser-on-loser. (I could play the ♦10, throwing a club, and later pitch a second club on the ♦9, which would

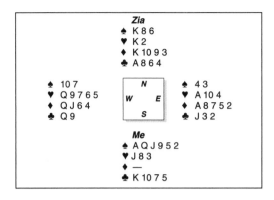

<pre>
            Zia
          ♠ K 8 6
          ♥ K 2
          ♦ K 10 9 3
          ♣ A 8 6 4
  ♠ 10 7   ♠ 4 3
  ♥ Q 9 7 6 5   N   ♥ A 10 4
  ♦ Q J 6 4   W   E   ♦ A 8 7 5 2
  ♣ Q 9   S   ♣ J 3 2
            Me
          ♠ A Q J 9 5 2
          ♥ J 8 3
          ♦ —
          ♣ K 10 7 5
</pre>

now be good.) I decided that East probably had the heart ace, so I ran the jack. When Leufkens failed to cover that was an overtrick. We won the event by two IMPs and, by a strange quirk of fate, if I had not stolen this trick Leufkens-Westra would have won the event. I was happy about this hand, not because it helped us to win, but because it meant that I was no longer scared to do what I thought was right, even if I risked looking foolish.

I love Chinese finesses, and I feel that they are frequently indicated as the 'percentage' play. Most experts won't even consider them unless they are certain no other play can succeed.

DEBBIE

Another learning milestone occurred when I met my wife, Debbie (then Debbie Zuckerberg — she won the World Junior Teams Championship at Ann Arbor in 1991). She made me see how much nonsense there was in the way I , and most other experts, thought about certain bidding situations. For example, we discussed help suit game tries. She asked me to name all the holdings on which I might make such a bid. Then she asked me to identify all the holdings which I considered 'good' or 'okay to accept' opposite a help suit game try. I now realized that it was unreasonable to make a help suit game try on both A108x and 8xxx, and then expect partner to know how to evaluate Q9x. The real answer is, firstly, to play the re-raise as a game try rather than as preemptive (so that the help suit game tries can remain pure), and secondly, to limit the possible holdings for a help suit game try to those which need a doubleton or less opposite. This, and other examples, taught me to work harder to weed out the rubbish from both my own and others' thoughts about bidding.

Debbie also taught me not to rush into taking control in slam auctions — something of which both Zia and I were frequently guilty. It *was* possible to have a sensible auction stopping at five-of-a-major, with slam not being reached because each player was aware that the other had failed to take control and, therefore, could not have enough for slam. (Having said this, it is a greater error not to take control when one has the right hand for it. Failing to do so is to invite disaster.)

TEMPERAMENT

So now I had acquired ability and confidence, but there was still one major area in which I was shockingly deficient. As I have said, there were usually fireworks when I played with Zia, and this detracted from my ability to focus. Worse still, I spent time at the table brooding over my errors on previous hands, or just simply analyzing them (the hands, not the errors). It was crucial to my improving my game that I stopped, or at least greatly reduced, this habit. One person was largely responsible for my being able to improve my focus — Bob Hamman.

I first played with Hamman in a pairs game in the 1991 Fall Nationals; I played again with him in the Blue Ribbon Pairs in 1993, which we won. What struck me most about him was his ability to focus on the hand he was playing. Nothing fazed him — he gave 100% until the last card was played. It didn't take a genius to see how much this quality was worth, so I tried to be the same. I remember during one session of the Blues: on the second board I made a sick/lazy bid and, as a result, we missed a laydown grand. In the past, I would have felt disgusted, and that would have been likely to affect my play; but I resolved to be tough, and played fine for the rest of the session. That felt so good I was almost glad I had made the sick bid!

Playing in the 1995 Spingold quarter-final, I had a total mind-loss on one hand. The very next deal:

Zia

- ♠ A 10 7 3
- ♥ J 4
- ♦ A 10 3
- ♣ A 5 3 2

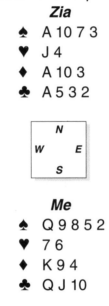

Me

- ♠ Q 9 8 5 2
- ♥ 7 6
- ♦ K 9 4
- ♣ Q J 10

North-South vul.

WEST	NORTH	EAST	SOUTH
1♥	dbl	4♥	4♠
all pass			

West won the first two tricks with the king and queen of hearts. East, who appeared to have the ace, asked for a diamond shift, and West duly led the diamond eight to trick three. What now?

West obviously had both black kings, so holding my black-suit losers to one was no problem. My diamond loser could go on the fourth club if that suit broke 3-3; if not, I would need an endplay. Also, there was the slight hope of picking up trumps.

Suddenly, I saw the perfect line — one which maximized both my legitimate and my deceptive chances. Playing low from dummy, I won East's ♦J with my king. Then I led the ♣Q which was covered by the king and ace. Returning to the ♣J, I now led the ♠Q, again covered by the king and ace (no jack). Next, I led a club from dummy. If clubs had been 3-3, I could now have conceded a trump and claimed. Also, if East had ruffed with an original holding of ♠Jx, he would have been endplayed. In fact, East discarded after protracted thought. I decided that he did not have the ♠J and, therefore, did not attempt to endplay him. West appeared to be 2-5-2-4, so I crossed to the diamond ace, ruffed the fourth club, and conceded a trump, endplaying West. The full deal:

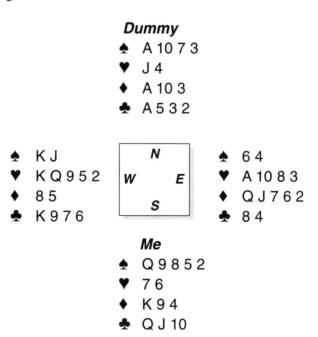

Dummy
♠ A 10 7 3
♥ J 4
♦ A 10 3
♣ A 5 3 2

♠ K J
♥ K Q 9 5 2
♦ 8 5
♣ K 9 7 6

N
W   E
S

♠ 6 4
♥ A 10 8 3
♦ Q J 7 6 2
♣ 8 4

Me
♠ Q 9 8 5 2
♥ 7 6
♦ K 9 4
♣ Q J 10

Yes, East made the losing play, but he didn't have a lock. I might have held, for example, the spade jack instead of the nine, and a low club instead of the ten. Then ruffing would have been fatal. Probably, East should have gone right, but the important aspect for me of this hand was my ability to focus, immediately after a mind-loss.

Another interesting thing I noticed when I partnered Hamman was that he never asked me why I had done what I did — *never*. On one hand from the 1994 World Pairs in Albuquerque, we were defending three notrump and I led a club. Dummy had ♣A8x and played small. Hamman followed with his singleton ten, and declarer won the queen. I won the diamond at trick two and, in perfect tempo, played the club king. Declarer's clubs were ♣QJ9x, so this was not a great success (although it did not actually cost a trick on the hand). Nothing was said (of course), but I could see Bob looking a little confused.

Later that night, we were sitting around in Nick Nickell's suite, and Hamman suddenly said to Nickell, "Michael made a great play today." He then proceeded to describe what had taken place on this hand. Nick thought for a few seconds and naturally asked me, "Why did you do that?" This was the situation from my viewpoint:

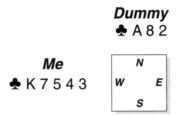

Dummy
♣ A 8 2

Me
♣ K 7 5 4 3

	N	
W		E
	S	

I had led the ♣4, and the trick went ♣2, ♣10, ♣Q. I won
trick two and had one more entry. In playing the ♣K now,
I hoped that partner had the jack, and that declarer would
duck — after all, he would think that I had the jack. Meanwhile, playing a low club would be ineffective if partner
had jack-ten doubleton, since declarer *would* duck. I also
knew that, if declarer had the jack, I was losing nothing
(unless he had four), since he was marked with the nine.
So I played the king. I was able to do this in tempo, because
I had been in a similar situation before:

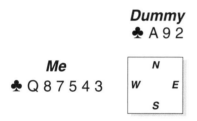

Dummy
♣ A 9 2

Me
♣ Q 8 7 5 4 3

Defending three notrump, I had led the ♣5, and the trick
had gone ♣2, ♣10, ♣K. I won some later trick and played
the club queen. Declarer naturally ducked, and the contract was defeated.

What impressed me was that Hamman, instead of asking me why I had done it, or assuming that I was mad, had
figured it out. He never asked me to explain anything. I
guess he has so much confidence in himself that he knows
he can figure out his partner's reasoning — and if it does-
n't make sense he concludes that his partner made a mistake. I admire that.

One of my biggest thrills was winning the 1996 Vanderbilt.
In the final we (myself, Zia, Seymon Deutsch, Chip Martel

and Lew Stansby) beat the dreaded Nickell team (Nickell-Freeman, Meckstroth-Rodwell, Hamman-Wolff) which had won the previous three Spingolds (defeating me twice in the finals and once in the semis), the previous three Reisingers, and the 1995 Bermuda Bowl. One of my greatest moments occurred during the third quarter:

Zia
- ♠ 10 7 5
- ♥ A K Q J 5
- ♦ Q 6 3
- ♣ 10 7

Me
- ♠ Q J 4 2
- ♥ 9
- ♦ K 8
- ♣ A K J 9 6 3

North-South vul.

Wolff WEST	Zia NORTH	Hamman EAST	Me SOUTH
		pass	1♣
pass	1♥	pass	1♠
pass	2♦[1]	dbl	3♣
pass	3♥	pass	3NT
all pass			

1. Fourth-suit forcing to game

Wolff led the diamond jack. It looked like it would be a fairly quick hand — if the club queen was right, I would probably make five or six; if it was wrong, I would probably go down three or four.

Once I won the diamond, should I cash the club ace before testing hearts? This would be correct if I had five heart tricks, but wrong if I had only four. Since I was assuming that East had four clubs, and he seemed to have at least five diamonds (and West had not overcalled 1♠), it was clear that I could not count on five heart tricks. Therefore, it would be wrong to cash the ♣A.

Was there any point in ducking the diamond? Only if diamonds were 6-2, and East had no entry. If the opponents cleared diamonds I would still go down one, losing two spades, two diamonds and a club; but that was a lot better than down four vulnerable.

Was there any downside to ducking? Apart from possible overtrick IMPs, only jack-ten doubleton in West with no entry in East — I would blow the contract in that case. It seemed worth the risk — especially so because either opponent might panic if East had no entry.

So, I let the jack win. Wolff started thinking, and the more he thought, the more I became convinced that he would *not* play another diamond. Eventually, he emerged with the heart eight. Now it was my turn to trance. I should have played a diamond now, assuming that West had everything, and I would almost certainly make even if he had five hearts. However, I actually cashed hearts (they broke) pitching a spade and three clubs. Wolff, who started with four hearts, pitched a spade on the fifth. Now I led a spade to the queen. Wolff won, and was stuck. Whatever he did, either the queen of diamonds would become my ninth trick, or he would be endplayed.

The full deal:

Dummy
- ♠ 10 7 5
- ♥ A K Q J 5
- ♦ Q 6 3
- ♣ 10 7

Wolff
- ♠ A K 9 6
- ♥ 10 8 6 2
- ♦ J 5
- ♣ Q 5 2

Hamman
- ♠ 8 3
- ♥ 7 4 3
- ♦ A 10 9 7 4 2
- ♣ 8 4

Me
- ♠ Q J 4 2
- ♥ 9
- ♦ K 8
- ♣ A K J 9 6 3

In the endgame, if Wolff cashed the other high spade, I would unblock the jack. If he then continued spades to knock out dummy's entry, I would cash the club ace-king, and play the diamond king, forcing Hamman to concede the ninth trick.

However, that was not my great moment.

A few hands later, I played 4♥ with a trump suit of ♥Q932 facing ♥AJ65. I guessed to play a heart to the ace dropping Hamman's stiff king offside, thus gaining a game swing.

However, that was not my great moment.

On the next deal the tray came through the screen showing that Zia had opened 1NT. And Hamman 'over-called' 1♠ — yes, *one* spade! He was so shaken by the events of this quarter that he had momentarily lost focus and had not seen the opening bid.

That was my great moment.

CHAPTER FOUR

MY FAVORITE HANDS

The following fifteen hands hold a special fascination for me. Each of them contains something which thrilled me at the time, and many of them continue to do so. I suggest that you take your time with them.

In fairness, you should know that they are not all 'real' problems. I define a real problem as one which, when you have solved it, you *know* you have solved it, and the solution is satisfying. (This is as opposed to real-life problems, which often have no 'answer' at all.)

Hold out on turning to the solutions (which can be found after all the hands) for as long as you can bear it!

Dummy

♠ 10 3 2
♥ A 4 2
♦ Q 4 3 2
♣ 10 3 2

```
        N
   W        E
        S
```

You

♠ A Q J
♥ K Q 3
♦ A K
♣ A Q J 5 4

WEST	NORTH	EAST	SOUTH
			2♣
3♠	pass[1]	pass	6NT
all pass			

1. Shows values

West leads the ♥J. Plan the play.

Dummy

♠ Q 9 6 2
♥ A
♦ Q 9
♣ K 9 8 5 4 2

You

♠ A 3
♥ J 8 5 2
♦ A K J 10 7 6 3
♣ —

WEST	NORTH	EAST	SOUTH
2♦[1]	pass	2♥	3NT
pass	4♣	pass	5♦
pass	6♦	dbl	all pass

1. Weak 2-bid in hearts or spades.

West leads the ♣J. Plan the play.

Dummy

♠ J 9 4 2
♥ A 7 2
♦ A 4
♣ A 6 5 2

```
      N
  W       E
      S
```

You

♠ K
♥ Q J 8 6 3
♦ J 9 7 2
♣ K 7 3

WEST	NORTH	EAST	SOUTH
	1♣	dbl	1♥
1♠	2♥	pass	3♦
pass	4♥	all pass	

West leads the ♠5 (fourth best). East wins and returns the ♥4. Plan the play.

Dummy

♠ A Q 9 2
♥ A J 9 2
♦ A 10 7 3
♣ 2

You

♠ K 10 7 6
♥ K 10
♦ K Q 5
♣ A K Q J

7NT by South. West leads the ♣10. Plan the play.

Dummy

♠ J 3 2
♥ K
♦ A J 7 4 2
♣ A Q 8 3

You

♠ 10 5 4
♥ A J 7 4 2
♦ K
♣ K 7 4 2

3NT by South. West, who passed originally, leads the ace, king, queen and a fourth spade, and then shifts to a heart. How do you plan to take nine tricks? (You discard a red card from each hand.)

Dummy
- ♠ 9 7 2
- ♥ J 5
- ♦ K 10 2
- ♣ A K 10 4 2

N
W   E
S

Zia

You
- ♠ K J 5
- ♥ Q 7 6 4 3
- ♦ 7 5 3
- ♣ J 5

WEST	EAST
	1♥
2♣	2NT
3NT	pass

You lead the ♥4, dummy plays the ♥5, partner the ♥K, and declarer the ♥A. Declarer, who happens to be none other than Zia Mahmood, crosses to the ♣A and plays a spade. Partner wins the ♠A and returns the ♥8, Zia following with the deuce. Plan the defense.

7. Magic Trick

Dummy
- ♠ Q 3
- ♥ K 2
- ♦ A 8 6 4
- ♣ A K 7 5 3

You
- ♠ A J 7 5 4 2
- ♥ A Q 6 3
- ♦ 7
- ♣ 8 4

A wheel comes off in the bidding and you arrive at 7♠. West leads the ♦Q. What chance is there to make this contract?

Dummy

♠ 10 9 8
♥ K
♦ Q J 5 4
♣ K 9 8 6 3

You

♠ A K
♥ A Q 10 6 5 2
♦ 8 7 2
♣ J 10

North-South vul.

WEST	NORTH	EAST	SOUTH
1♠	pass	2♠	3♥
pass	4♥	dbl	all pass

West leads the ♦K, East playing the ♦3. West switches to the ♠3. Plan the play.

Dummy
♠ A Q 5 4
♥ Q J 2
♦ A 9 3
♣ A 9 3

N	**You**
	♠ K J 7 3 2
W E	♥ K 5
	♦ K 5 2
S	♣ 7 5 2

NORTH	SOUTH
	2♥
4♥	pass

Partner leads the ♠6. Declarer plays low from dummy. Plan the defense.

Dummy

♠ K 8 4 2
♥ J 5 3
♦ A 8 6 3
♣ 9 4

You

♠ 9 7
♥ A K 10 9 6 2
♦ 9
♣ A 10 7 3

NORTH	SOUTH
	1♥
2♥	4♥
pass	

Playing rubber bridge, and feeling 'in the zone', you bid an exuberant 4♥. After all, you *do* have the ♦9. West leads the ♥4. Can you *play* in the zone, too?

Dummy
♠ K 10 2
♥ A 6 4
♦ Q J 9
♣ 7 6 4 2

You
♠ A Q 9 8 6 3
♥ Q 10 2
♦ A 5 3
♣ K

Neither vul.

WEST	NORTH	EAST	SOUTH
			1♠
pass	2♠	pass	pass
3♥	3♠	4♣	4♠
dbl	all pass		

Playing rubber bridge against Zia on your left, you take an unusual position. You pass 2♠ smoothly, knowing that Zia would rather settle down and get married than pass out this auction. Then, when partner shows a maximum, you bid game, hoping that the extra knowledge will prove useful. Zia leads the ♣10. East wins the ace and returns the ♥8. Plan the play.

Dummy
- ♠ A 5
- ♥ A 9 4
- ♦ A 10 9 5 4
- ♣ A 9 4

You
- ♠ 9 2
- ♥ K Q 7 6 2
- ♦ 8 7 3 2
- ♣ Q 5

East-West vul.

WEST	NORTH	EAST	SOUTH
1♠	dbl	pass	3♥
4♣	4♥	all pass	

West leads the ♠K. Plan the play.

Dummy
- ♠ A Q 2
- ♥ A Q 2
- ♦ 7 6 5
- ♣ K J 9 7

```
      N
  W       E
      S
```

You
- ♠ J 5 3
- ♥ J 5 3
- ♦ A 4 3
- ♣ A Q 10 8

WEST	NORTH	EAST	SOUTH
		1♦	pass
pass	dbl	pass	2NT
pass	3NT	all pass	

West leads the ♦8, East playing the ♦9. Plan the play.

Dummy

♠ K 4 2
♥ A Q 5 3
♦ 5 4 3 2
♣ 6 4

You

♠ A Q J 10 9
♥ K J
♦ 6
♣ A K Q 5 3

After West opens the bidding 4♦, you arrive in 6♠. West leads the ♦K. East wins the ace (perforce) and switches to a trump, on which West discards a diamond. The fortunate diamond position has allowed you to survive the bad trump break. How do you continue?

Dummy

♠ Q 5 4 3 2
♥ 7 4 2
♦ 5 3
♣ A 8 5

You

♠ A J 7
♥ A K Q J 10 3
♦ 4
♣ K Q 7

The defenders lead two rounds of diamonds against your inferior 6♥ contract. What are your chances of making twelve tricks?

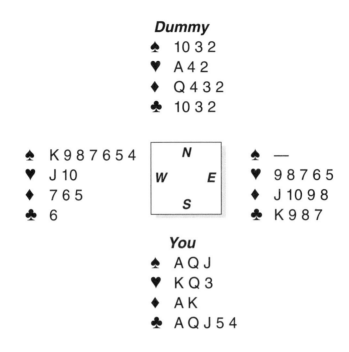

Dummy
- ♠ 10 3 2
- ♥ A 4 2
- ♦ Q 4 3 2
- ♣ 10 3 2

West:
- ♠ K 9 8 7 6 5 4
- ♥ J 10
- ♦ 7 6 5
- ♣ 6

East:
- ♠ —
- ♥ 9 8 7 6 5
- ♦ J 10 9 8
- ♣ K 9 8 7

You
- ♠ A Q J
- ♥ K Q 3
- ♦ A K
- ♣ A Q J 5 4

This looks to be a simple hand — at first. Clearly, the club finesse is required and, equally clearly, there will be no difficulty if clubs break 3-2. If East has four or five clubs he will be squeezed, providing that he has at least four diamonds; and if he has fewer, the contract is unlikely to be made in practice. So, what's the problem? The problem is that East will unguard *diamonds* and declarer will be subjected to a one-suit suicide squeeze on the fourth diamond! He will be unable to discard a low or middle club without conceding a trick to East.

The trick, strangely, is to 'lose' one of your tricks. Carefully win the ♥K, cash the ♦AK and play the ♠AQ. West wins (if he doesn't, you simply concede a club) and returns the ♥10. Win the ace, *unblocking the queen*, and cash the ♦Q, jettisoning the ♠J. Follow with the ♠10, and now East is squeezed in *three* suits! He can never pitch a club or declarer discards his heart and claims. He does best to throw a diamond, but now the thirteenth diamond forces him to part with his last heart. Now declarer finesses the club and, crossing back to the 'carefully' preserved ♥4, repeats the club finesse to make twelve tricks.

I solved this par hand in 1977 when it was given to me as a single-dummy problem. About twelve years later it was presented to me as a double-dummy problem by Vinny Bartone, but with all the small cards shown as x's. After about a minute I recognized the problem and said to him, "Ask whoever gave you this problem if dummy's hearts are ♥A42."

"Why?" he asked.

"Just do it," I said. A little later, Vinny came to me and said, "You're right, but how did you know? What possible difference can it make?"

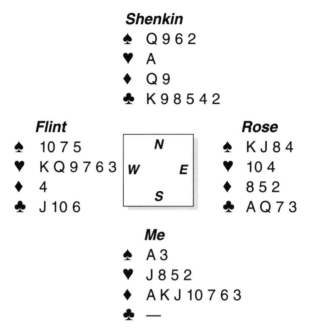

Shenkin
- ♠ Q 9 6 2
- ♥ A
- ♦ Q 9
- ♣ K 9 8 5 4 2

Flint
- ♠ 10 7 5
- ♥ K Q 9 7 6 3
- ♦ 4
- ♣ J 10 6

Rose
- ♠ K J 8 4
- ♥ 10 4
- ♦ 8 5 2
- ♣ A Q 7 3

Me
- ♠ A 3
- ♥ J 8 5 2
- ♦ A K J 10 7 6 3
- ♣ —

I played this hand in the 1976 British Trials against Jeremy Flint and Irving Rose, two of the greatest players ever to hail from Great Britain.

After a few minutes thought, I decided on the following plan: ruff the opening lead, heart to the ace, ruff three more clubs while ruffing two hearts, and play all the trumps. This was the position I hoped for when I played the last trump:

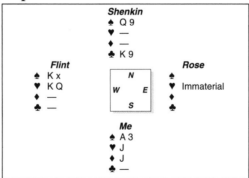

Shenkin
- ♠ Q 9
- ♥ —
- ♦ —
- ♣ K 9

Flint
- ♠ K x
- ♥ K Q
- ♦ —
- ♣ —

Rose
- ♠
- ♥ Immaterial
- ♦
- ♣

Me
- ♠ A 3
- ♥ J
- ♦ J
- ♣ —

When I played the last trump, Flint would be forced to discard a heart and could now be endplayed. I had the feeling that Rose was more likely to hold the spade king because of his double, but what could I do? Beyond playing him for three clubs and 2-2 diamonds, I couldn't make the hand if he had the king of spades, and that seemed like too much to play for. However, the cards were distributed as in the full-hand diagram above, so down I went.

As I was walking disconsolately away from the table, Martin Hoffman came running up to me.

"Six diamonds was laydown," he said. "All you have to do is play the hand in the order that you did, but ruff the four clubs with higher diamonds. Then, three rounds of diamonds endplays East."

Of course, you can see that East can foil this plan by retaining the deuce of diamonds, but that would not be an easy defense to find at the table, even for Irving Rose. And West might have held the bare deuce. If I had held the deuce, it would have been a perfect hand and I would have bungled it!

I felt crushed. I prided myself on seeing par hand positions such as this and, despite several minutes thought, had missed it completely. I made a vow to myself that the next time the opportunity for this type of play arose, I would spot it.

Hamman
- ♠ J 9 4 2
- ♥ A 7 2
- ♦ A 4
- ♣ A 6 5 2

Deas

- ♠ 10 8 6 5 3   ♠ A Q 7
- ♥ K 5   ♥ 10 9 4
- ♦ 8 6 3   ♦ K Q 10 5
- ♣ J 10 8   ♣ Q 9 4

```
        N
    W       E
        S
```

Me
- ♠ K
- ♥ Q J 8 6 3
- ♦ J 9 7 2
- ♣ K 7 3

Playing in the 1991 *Bridge Today* All-Star Individual with Bob Hamman, I reached a very pushy 4♥ contract. When East, Lynn Deas, returned a heart I was caught in a quandary. It was dollars-to-doughnuts that she had the king on the bidding, but I couldn't see how I was going to make the hand if she did (I needed her to have AQx in spades and only three hearts, so she rated to have at least four diamonds for her takeout double; thus KQx in diamonds was impossible). However, not wanting to go down extras, and hoping that I was missing something (or that they would somehow misdefend), I played the queen and was soon down one. Obviously, had I played low I would have made the hand (ruff a spade, duck a diamond, etc.).

I was mad at myself because I knew that, given my analysis, I *should* have played low. After the session I was determined to discover if playing the queen could ever be right. After much thought I came up with this scenario:

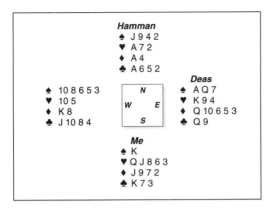

Win the heart queen and play the *nine of diamonds* (an avoidance play). East wins and returns a club (best). (If East plays another low heart, win the jack, draw trumps, ruff a spade, diamond ace, ruff a spade, and concede a diamond, pitching your club loser on the spade jack.) Now, club ace, spade ruff, heart ace, spade ruff, club king, diamond ace, leaves:

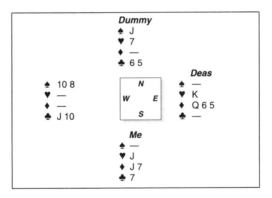

When the spade jack is played from dummy East is finished. If she ruffs, she is endplayed; if she discards, I pitch a club and elope with two ruffs.

So which hand is more likely? I don't know, but this is certainly more aesthetically pleasing. In any event, I was delighted to have proved that my play was not 'nullo' — and to have demonstrated once again that the 'Curse of Scotland' is the most important card in the deck.

Dummy

♠ A Q 9 2
♥ A J 9 2
♦ A 10 7 3
♣ 2

♠ 5   ♠ J 8 4 3
♥ 8 6 5 4 3   ♥ Q 7
♦ 8 4   ♦ J 9 6 2
♣ 10 9 7 5 3   ♣ 8 6 4

W   N   E   S

You

♠ K 10 7 6
♥ K 10
♦ K Q 5
♣ A K Q J

At first glance it feels as if there should be a sure-trick solution to this hand. Perhaps the most natural attempt is to play a spade to the ace and another to the king, the principle being that you claim unless West shows out; and if he does you make on a double squeeze, unless East controls diamonds as well as spades. However, even in this case, you can still fall back on the heart finesse which is now well over 50% — pretty good, huh? That must all add up to a more than 95% line. But you can do better!

My preferred order for the *100% play* is to win the first four tricks with aces. Then, cash the king and queen of diamonds and run the clubs discarding three hearts from dummy, leaving the position at the top of the next page.

Dummy
♠ Q 9 2
♥ —
♦ 10
♣ —

You
♠ K 10 7
♥ K
♦ —
♣ —

Now lead the heart king discarding the diamond ten —
it doesn't matter who has what — and we are basically
down to two possibilities. If anyone is still holding the diamond jack (or a club) he cannot also have the remaining
spades. If East discarded the diamond jack at trick ten he
must have three spades left.

The apparent 'extra chances' given by the ♥J10 and the
♦10 were a mirage.

Dummy

♠ J 3 2
♥ K
♦ A J 7 4 2
♣ A Q 8 3

You

♠ 10 5 4
♥ A J 7 4 2
♦ K
♣ K 7 4 2

No normal squeeze can operate with these cards due to lack of communication. East must hold at least one red queen, since West passed originally. He will hold both queens about one third of the time. The obvious hope is to find someone with Qx in a red suit — about 17%. However, you can improve your chances to about '31% minus' (one sixth of the remainder, minus the chance that East is extremely alert).

Win the heart and lead the *eight of clubs* to the king. Cash the diamond king and the heart ace, pitching a diamond. Cross to the ace and queen of clubs and cash the diamond ace, pitch-

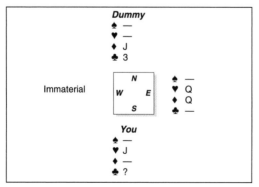

ing a heart (see left). When the ♣3 is played, which queen should East hold on to? Only if he has been watching very carefully will this be anything other than a guess.

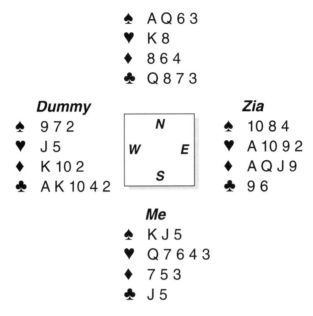

♠ A Q 6 3
♥ K 8
♦ 8 6 4
♣ Q 8 7 3

Dummy
♠ 9 7 2
♥ J 5
♦ K 10 2
♣ A K 10 4 2

Zia
♠ 10 8 4
♥ A 10 9 2
♦ A Q J 9
♣ 9 6

Me
♠ K J 5
♥ Q 7 6 4 3
♦ 7 5 3
♣ J 5

As soon as Zia played a spade from dummy it was clear to me that he was wide open in spades. He hoped that we would continue hearts, and he would make three tricks there plus six or seven in the minors. Did he really think this could work against *me*? I won the ♥Q and, giving him a look which mingled contempt with pity, I banged down the ♠K ready to cash out. Unfortunately, the actual deal was not quite as diagrammed above — the play to this trick went seven, three, *queen*. Oh no! I had failed to realize the necessity of unblocking the ♠J earlier! Zia's actual hand:

♠ Q 4   ♥ A 10 9 2   ♦ A Q J 9 4   ♣ 9 6

This was not a fair problem, since the fatal mistake was presented as a *fait accompli*. However, to present it as 'what do you play under the spade ace?' would make it too easy. Would you have found the winning defense? Award yourself eleven out of ten if you thought of it before seeing the 'solution'.

Dummy
- ♠ Q 3
- ♥ K 2
- ♦ A 8 6 4
- ♣ A K 7 5 3

West
- ♠ 10 9 6
- ♥ J 8 5
- ♦ Q J 10 2
- ♣ Q 10 2

East
- ♠ K 8
- ♥ 10 9 7 4
- ♦ K 9 5 3
- ♣ J 9 6

Me
- ♠ A J 7 5 4 2
- ♥ A Q 6 3
- ♦ 7
- ♣ 8 4

This is not so much a difficult play problem as it is an astonishing hand. If you tried to sneak the spade queen through because this hand 'can't be made any other way', you had better think again. Win the diamond ace and ruff a diamond. Use the ace and king of clubs to ruff two more diamonds, cross to the heart king and ruff a club. Cash the ace and queen of hearts leaving:

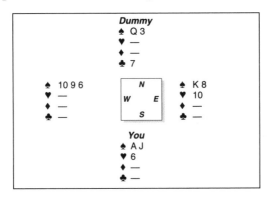

Now lead the heart and a 'sure' trump trick disappears — ruff with the ♠Q, and finesse the jack coming back.. When I first saw this hand I was amazed. I knew about the Devil's Coup, but this seemed to contravene the natural laws of physics. Even a trump lead makes no difference — the trump trick simply evaporates in a two-card ending instead.

It only takes one hand such as this to start me wondering how many more "unmakable" hands can be made.

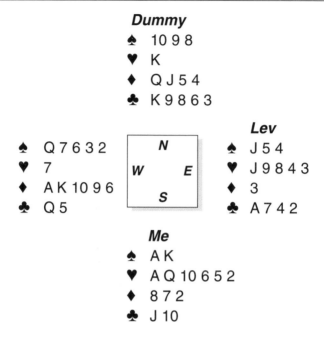

Dummy
- ♠ 10 9 8
- ♥ K
- ♦ Q J 5 4
- ♣ K 9 8 6 3

Lev
- ♠ J 5 4
- ♥ J 9 8 4 3
- ♦ 3
- ♣ A 7 4 2

(West)
- ♠ Q 7 6 3 2
- ♥ 7
- ♦ A K 10 9 6
- ♣ Q 5

Me
- ♠ A K
- ♥ A Q 10 6 5 2
- ♦ 8 7 2
- ♣ J 10

This hand occurred in a money IMPs game in New York in 1992. Winning the spade, I led a heart to the king, returned to a spade, and cashed the ♥A getting the bad news. I now led the ♣10 and West played low (had West covered, East could win and return a club for two down). East, Sam Lev, ducked the first club, won the second and returned a spade. Now I was able to ruff and endplay East in trumps for down one.

That night I realized something about this hand was bothering me. What if I had cashed the spade *before* crossing to the ♥K? Then I could have ruffed a spade before cashing a high trump and sneaking through the ♣10, thus depriving Lev of an exit card after he won the second club. He would be forced to exit a trump and now ten, queen, and another trump would endplay him to make four! The only defense would be for him to unblock in trumps, letting me win all the trumps, but allowing West to take the last two tricks with the ♦A and a spade.

But wait! I could lead the ♥5 to the king and ruff a spade with the ♥6 and — oh no, my vow! Do I have to wait another sixteen years for a chance to cure this particular blind spot?

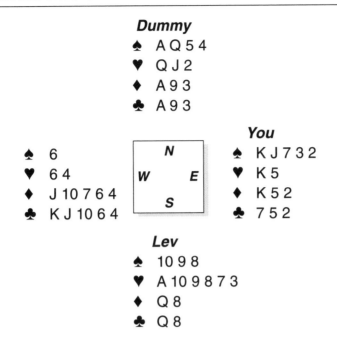

Dummy
- ♠ A Q 5 4
- ♥ Q J 2
- ♦ A 9 3
- ♣ A 9 3

You
- ♠ K J 7 3 2
- ♥ K 5
- ♦ K 5 2
- ♣ 7 5 2

West:
- ♠ 6
- ♥ 6 4
- ♦ J 10 7 6 4
- ♣ K J 10 6 4

Lev
- ♠ 10 9 8
- ♥ A 10 9 8 7 3
- ♦ Q 8
- ♣ Q 8

If you thought this was one of those hands where you should win the spade king to deceive declarer and talk him out of the trump finesse — I'm sorry, but declarer would know that your partner's lead was not from ♠J7632. Instead, you must give partner a spade ruff and take two more tricks in the minors. It won't matter that a diamond return by West after the spade ruff sets up the queen, because declarer cannot afford to duck it, else he loses another ruff.

So, East won the spade jack and returned the seven, suit-preference. West ruffed and returned a diamond but declarer, Sam Lev, rose with the ace, drew two trumps, crossed to the club ace, and reeled off the trumps leaving the position on the next page.

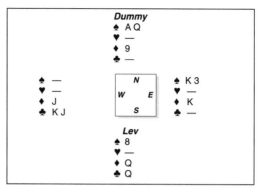

Reading the position correctly, Lev exited with a diamond, endplaying East.

It struck me as interesting that, if East had asked for a *club* return instead of a diamond after the spade ruff, then Lev would probably have gone down. In fact, the more I thought about it, the more I realized that East *should* have asked for a club. If declarer has no queens it doesn't matter and, if he has one queen, you will at least break even, since he will inevitably play for the strip squeeze.

And, you may score a huge gain if his minors are, e.g., ♦ Qx ♣Jx, because he may still try to throw you in with a club (assuming that your partner cooperates and returns a *low* club). Furthermore, you will also gain when declarer's minors are ♦xx ♣QJ, or ♦x ♣Q10x, since he will almost certainly go wrong. Of course, it goes without saying that the quicker you can figure out to ask for a club, the more situations there are where you are likely to gain.

Dummy
- ♠ K 8 4 2
- ♥ J 5 3
- ♦ A 8 6 3
- ♣ 9 4

West:
- ♠ Q 10 6 3
- ♥ 8 7 4
- ♦ K J 4
- ♣ K J 6

East:
- ♠ A J 5
- ♥ Q
- ♦ Q 10 7 5 2
- ♣ Q 8 5 2

	N	
W		E
	S	

Me
- ♠ 9 7
- ♥ A K 10 9 6 2
- ♦ 9
- ♣ A 10 7 3

This hand was a pleasurable experience for me — one of those rare moments when I felt I had done something good.

At trick two I crossed to the diamond ace and ruffed a diamond (the key play), and then played a low club. If East had held three clubs to two honors, plus a stiff heart, I would have been cold; but West won the club jack and returned a second trump, on which East naturally (but fatally) discarded a diamond.

Winning in dummy, I ruffed another diamond, played the ace of clubs and ruffed a club, and ruffed dummy's last diamond leaving the position illustrated on the next page.

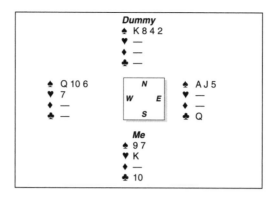

Dummy
♠ K 8 4 2
♥ —
♦ —
♣ —

♠ Q 10 6   ♠ A J 5
♥ 7   ♥ —
♦ —   ♦ —
♣ —   ♣ Q

Me
♠ 9 7
♥ K
♦ —
♣ 10

After drawing the last trump I played a club to East, who now regretted having parted with his 'useless' diamond. Do you think you would have found a spade pitch with the East hand? Then I would probably still choose to play the hand the same way, gaining when East has 4-1-4-4 with the spade ace, but going down in a 'cooler' when East has 5-1-3-4 with no spade ace. The former is a more likely mathematical possibility.

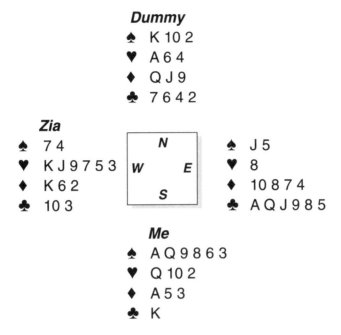

Dummy
- ♠ K 10 2
- ♥ A 6 4
- ♦ Q J 9
- ♣ 7 6 4 2

Zia
- ♠ 7 4
- ♥ K J 9 7 5 3
- ♦ K 6 2
- ♣ 10 3

- ♠ J 5
- ♥ 8
- ♦ 10 8 7 4
- ♣ A Q J 9 8 5

Me
- ♠ A Q 9 8 6 3
- ♥ Q 10 2
- ♦ A 5 3
- ♣ K

This hand took place in a rubber bridge game in 1989 in New York. On the bidding, I felt sure that Zia held the diamond king. I covered with the ten of hearts and took Zia's jack with the ace. I ruffed a club with the spade eight, cashed the ace and king of trumps, and ruffed another club. Then, since it looked as if Zia was 2-6-3-2, I tried a low diamond. Zia laughed as he put up the king and exited with a diamond, saying, "You can't endplay me." True, but I could (and did) endplay his partner with the *fourth* round of clubs.

This was a fairly simple hand, but I liked that I saw the end position from the beginning, while the rest of the table didn't see it until it happened.

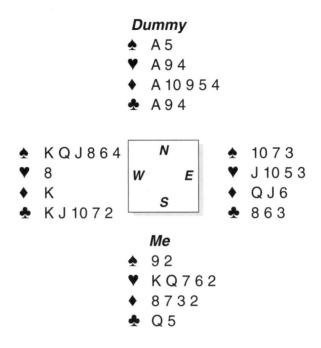

Dummy
- ♠ A 5
- ♥ A 9 4
- ♦ A 10 9 5 4
- ♣ A 9 4

West:
- ♠ K Q J 8 6 4
- ♥ 8
- ♦ K
- ♣ K J 10 7 2

East:
- ♠ 10 7 3
- ♥ J 10 5 3
- ♦ Q J 6
- ♣ 8 6 3

Me
- ♠ 9 2
- ♥ K Q 7 6 2
- ♦ 8 7 3 2
- ♣ Q 5

I played this hand in the 1976 *Sunday Times* Invitational, in London. I let the ♠K hold and won the spade continuation. I played the ♥A and, noting happily the fall of the eight, ran the nine. When West pitched a spade, I paused.

Clearly West was 6-5, at least, to bid this way vulnerable; and if he wasn't 6-1-1-5, I had no chance. The danger now was that East would win the first diamond and shoot through a club before I had time to establish the fifth diamond for a discard. Therefore, I needed West to hold the bare ♦K so that I could lose the first diamond to him. I then realized that drawing further trumps would afford West the opportunity to disgorge the offending monarch. Therefore, at trick four, I led a low diamond from dummy and was fortunate to find the existing distribution.

Immediately after the hand, I was aware that I had bungled the play. By playing trumps first I had unnecessarily given West one chance to discard that king. Precisely the same reasoning that I used at trick four could, and should, have been used at trick two — a low diamond at once was the correct play. If West won and persisted with a third spade, I could ruff in hand discarding a club from dummy. Then, heart to the ace, ♥9 covered, diamond to the ace, finesse the ♥7, and draw the last trump discarding dummy's other low club. Finally, concede a diamond to East who cannot have any spades left, and must, therefore, concede the last three tricks to the dummy.

Dummy
- ♠ A Q 2
- ♥ A Q 2
- ♦ 7 6 5
- ♣ K J 9 7

West		East
♠ 9 8 6 4		♠ K 10 7
♥ 9 8 6		♥ K 10 7 4
♦ 8 2		♦ K Q J 10 9
♣ 6 5 4 3		♣ 2

You
- ♠ J 5 3
- ♥ J 5 3
- ♦ A 4 3
- ♣ A Q 10 8

Over the years, I have had a good deal of fun giving this par hand to various experts. Typically, their answers take the following course: after a little thought they say, "I duck the first diamond, win the second, and cash four clubs. What does East come down to?"

"Kx in both majors and three diamonds," I answer.

"Then I throw East in with a diamond."

"Okay," I reply, "East cashes two more diamonds. What do you pitch from both hands?"

"Well, I... no... hmm... I can discard the queen of... hmm ... no. Wait a minute, I cash only *three* clubs before end-playing East."

"Okay, so what are your pitches?"

"I throw... a club and... a spade from dummy and a... spade and a heart from hand."

"Then East exits a spade and you must lose a heart."

"I guess that's right... wait a minute, *now* I've got it. I cash only *two* clubs before throwing East in. Now I can discard two clubs from dummy and a low card in each major from hand."

"East returns from a Kxx major suit after cashing his diamonds."

"Okay, so I win the jack and cash two more clubs squeezing East in the majors."

"The squeeze will not operate because your communication is blocked."

"There is only a single chance to make this hand," I quickly say before the expert can 'solve' the problem. Duck the first diamond, win the second and cash *one* club. Throw East in, discarding two clubs from dummy (leaving a fluid position) and a low card in each major from hand (East cannot help himself by not cashing his diamonds). Win the jack of whichever major East returns and *cross to the other ace* (a Vienna Coup) leaving, for example:

Overtake the club king and cash the remaining clubs throwing hearts from dummy — East is caught in a major-suit squeeze.

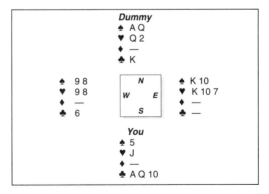

"I knew it was something like that, I almost got it ."

"Yes, you nearly had it the third time."

Dummy
- ♠ K 4 2
- ♥ A Q 5 3
- ♦ 5 4 3 2
- ♣ 6 4

You
- ♠ A Q J 10 9
- ♥ K J
- ♦ 6
- ♣ A K Q 5 3

Astute observers will have noticed there are no opposing cards in the diagrammed solution. That is because there is no appropriate East-West distribution for this sure-trick par problem (assuming 7-1 diamonds).

Since East has six cards in the pointed suits he cannot control both hearts and clubs. Therefore the hand must be makable by squeezing West between diamonds and a rounded suit. But which one? If you draw trumps and unfortunately guess to cash the suit which West holds, the squeeze will not operate. Meanwhile, it would also be nice if we could safely ruff a club in dummy.

The solution is as follows: since West has seven diamonds he cannot also hold seven hearts. Therefore, it must be safe to cash *one* heart. In the (unlikely) event that West shows out, cash the heart jack, cross to the spade king, pitch two clubs on the ace-queen of hearts, draw trumps and claim. If West follows to one heart he can no longer hold six clubs, so it must be safe to cash one of those. If West shows out, ruff a club in dummy, draw trumps, and discard the other club loser on a heart. If West follows to one club, East must have at least one more heart, so play a second heart. Getting the idea? If West shows out, cross to the spade king etc., and if West follows, play the king of clubs. If West shows out, cash the club queen and crossruff. If West follows, ruff a club high, draw trumps and claim (clubs *must* have broken no worse than 4-2).

So you see, this was not a squeeze hand, but a counting hand. This elegant 'see-saw' position was first shown to me in 1975 by Victor Silverstone.

Dummy
♠ Q 5 4 3 2
♥ 7 4 2
♦ 5 3
♣ A 8 5

♠ K   N   ♠ 10 9 8 6
♥ 9 8   W   E   ♥ 6 5
♦ K Q 10 7 6 2   ♦ A J 9 8
♣ J 9 4 2   S   ♣ 10 6 3

Declarer
♠ A J 7
♥ A K Q J 10 3
♦ 4
♣ K Q 7

It seems that the only chance is to find East with the sin-gleton or doubleton spade king but, in fact, at trick one, you can *claim* against a singleton king with West also. How?

This hand was played in a high-stakes rubber bridge game in London against Howard Cohen. The singleton king was indeed offside (otherwise this hand would prob-ably have been forgotten forever), and declarer duly went down; but later that night he figured out how he *should* have made the hand.

The solution is as follows: ruff the diamond and play five rounds of hearts discarding two spades from dummy. Cash three clubs ending in dummy to leave this (apparent-ly) simple end-position:

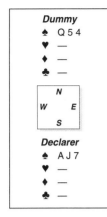

Dummy
♠ Q 5 4
♥ —
♦ —
♣ —

	N	
W		E
	S	

Declarer
♠ A J 7
♥ —
♦ —
♣ —

Now lead a small spade from dummy and, if East never discarded a spade, take the normal finesse. But, if East *did* throw a spade, play a spade to the ace. Why? Because East would never throw a spade(s) to come down to Kx. So, if he pitches one, the only chance is that he was *forced* to pitch one, as he would have been on the actual layout.

Yes, I know that East could defeat you an extra trick by discarding down to Kx; but firstly, he wouldn't, and secondly, who cares? In fact, it is precisely because you are certain to go down two if the spade king is wrong, that you would never play the hand this way — unless you saw the reason to do so.

This is my favorite hand of all time (so far!). I failed to solve it when I was given it as a problem and nobody I have ever presented it to has solved it. Some experts have failed to solve it when I have presented it a second time (after a suitable time lapse). One world champion failed to solve it *three times* over a ten-year period. Unfortunately, the hand has appeared in print before (*The Bridge World*), and has been substantially publicized by me, so it may not have been new to you.

Dummy
A J 10 x

	N	
W		E
	S	

Declarer
K x

As a practical matter, one should be aware of this analogous situation. If you reach a four-card ending and West has discarded from this suit, consider whether he was being helpful, or was *forced* to discard one from xxxxx.

CHAPTER FIVE

MAJOR REGRETS

IF ONLY...

The following four hands are those which I found, over the years, to be the most upsetting — for widely differing reasons. Three of them cost, or played a big part in costing, a major event.

The mistakes which bother me the most are always those which come as a result of my overly pessimistic outlook. That pessimism is sometimes about the lie of the opposing cards, and other times just a mistrust of my own feelings, i.e., thinking that whatever I do will be wrong. It is certainly not necessarily correct to go against one's own nature, but it is vitally important to be cognizant of it.

See whether you can do better than I did.

Hand 1. You hold

$$\spadesuit\ K\ 7\ 2 \quad \heartsuit\ A\ Q\ 8\ 4\ 2 \quad \diamondsuit\ Q\ 10\ 7\ 2 \quad \clubsuit\ J$$

LHO opens a Precision 2♣, with everybody vulnerable. After two passes you balance with a double, and LHO redoubles. Partner bids 2♠ and RHO bids 2NT. LHO raises to 3NT which partner doubles, ending the auction. What do you lead?

Hand 2. You hold

$$\spadesuit\ 7\ 5 \quad \heartsuit\ 9\ 8\ 2 \quad \diamondsuit\ K\ 10\ 8\ 6\ 5\ 2 \quad \clubsuit\ Q\ 9$$

RHO opens 1♥, and rebids 4♥ over LHO's 1♠ response. LHO cue-bids 5♣, and RHO's 6♥ bid concludes the auction. What is your lead?

Hand 3.

Dummy
- ♠ K 9 3
- ♥ 6
- ♦ A J 8 2
- ♣ A Q 10 6 4

```
      N
   W     E
      S
```

You
- ♠ A J
- ♥ A J 8 2
- ♦ K 9 7 5 3
- ♣ 7 5

WEST	NORTH	EAST	SOUTH
	1♣	1♥	2♦
pass	3♥	pass	3♠
pass	4♦	pass	4NT
pass	5♥	dbl	6♦
all pass			

West leads the ♥9 (doubleton at most). Plan the play.

Hand 4.

Dummy

♠ 8 6 4
♥ K 5 3
♦ 2
♣ A J 10 7 6 3

You

♠ —
♥ A J 10 8 6 2
♦ A J 10 9 4 3
♣ 8

WEST	NORTH	EAST	SOUTH
			1♥
1♠	2♠	4♠	6♥
pass[1]	pass	pass	

1. After some hesitation

West leads the club king. Plan the play.

Hand 1.

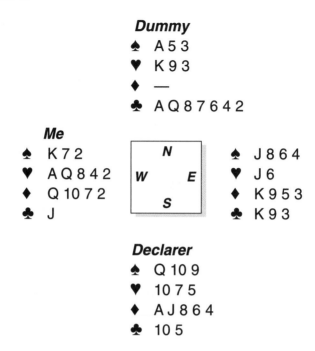

Dummy
- ♠ A 5 3
- ♥ K 9 3
- ♦ —
- ♣ A Q 8 7 6 4 2

Me
- ♠ K 7 2
- ♥ A Q 8 4 2
- ♦ Q 10 7 2
- ♣ J

- ♠ J 8 6 4
- ♥ J 6
- ♦ K 9 5 3
- ♣ K 9 3

Declarer
- ♠ Q 10 9
- ♥ 10 7 5
- ♦ A J 8 6 4
- ♣ 10 5

This hand occurred during the late stages of the British Trials for the 1976 World Team Olympiad. Had I led a heart (as I believe I should have) my team would have won — and I would have gone to Monte Carlo. Even a diamond lead would have sufficed, providing that partner holds up till the third club, since dummy can now be strip-squeezed and thrown in with a spade. On a heart lead, declarer would have to play almost double-dummy, just to go two down. I led a spade, and declarer wound up with an over-trick. And I wound up back in Glasgow.

Hand 2.

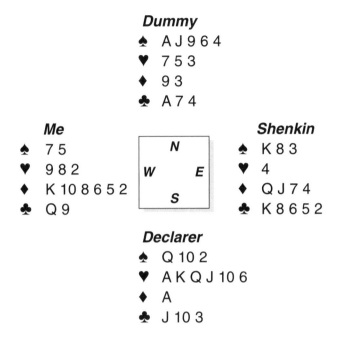

Dummy
- ♠ A J 9 6 4
- ♥ 7 5 3
- ♦ 9 3
- ♣ A 7 4

Me
- ♠ 7 5
- ♥ 9 8 2
- ♦ K 10 8 6 5 2
- ♣ Q 9

Shenkin
- ♠ K 8 3
- ♥ 4
- ♦ Q J 7 4
- ♣ K 8 6 5 2

Declarer
- ♠ Q 10 2
- ♥ A K Q J 10 6
- ♦ A
- ♣ J 10 3

This was the penultimate deal which I played in the 1978 Cavendish Invitational. Barnet Shenkin and I were leading entering the final session, but things had been a little rocky for us — we needed to beat this hand to win the event.

Barnet had not doubled 5♣, but I knew that declarer was prepared for a diamond lead. It felt as if I had to attack, but neither minor looked promising. For a diamond to work, I needed Barnet to have the ♦Q and neither opponent to have a singleton. For a club to be successful, partner needed the ♣K, but he hadn't doubled 5♣. Perhaps that was because he had the ♦Q with *fewer* diamonds, and did not want to steer me away from a diamond lead if I had the ♦K and declarer had a stiff club. Still, although I felt a club was more likely to work, I hated the idea of leading a club after partner's non-double, and finding that it was wrong. So, I led a diamond... and we came second.

Hand 3.

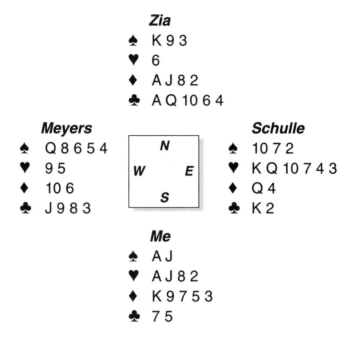

Zia
- ♠ K 9 3
- ♥ 6
- ♦ A J 8 2
- ♣ A Q 10 6 4

Meyers
- ♠ Q 8 6 5 4
- ♥ 9 5
- ♦ 10 6
- ♣ J 9 8 3

Schulle
- ♠ 10 7 2
- ♥ K Q 10 7 4 3
- ♦ Q 4
- ♣ K 2

Me
- ♠ A J
- ♥ A J 8 2
- ♦ K 9 7 5 3
- ♣ 7 5

I played this hand against Jill Meyers and Kay Schulle in an early round of the 1990 Vanderbilt. I felt that I would have no problem if I picked up the diamonds; but if I mis-guessed them I would need a black-suit finesse plus some care in the timing, since the bidding made it very likely that East had the ♣K. Yet it was the bidding that made me think that the spade finesse was due to fail. I knew that I, as East, would never double 5♥ holding the ♠Q, knowing that dummy had a stiff heart. Therefore, I felt that the 'right' play was to lead the ♠J planning to run it! This would be legitimately successful if East had ♠10x, and would also win when West failed to cover. I wasn't worried about what Zia, my partner, would say (he heartily approves of all such swindles); but I thought my teammates might not under-stand if this play failed. So I finessed the second round of diamonds and went down one. I deeply regret *not knowing* if the swindle would have worked.

Hand 4.

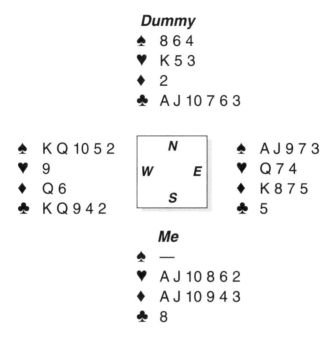

Dummy
- ♠ 8 6 4
- ♥ K 5 3
- ♦ 2
- ♣ A J 10 7 6 3

West
- ♠ K Q 10 5 2
- ♥ 9
- ♦ Q 6
- ♣ K Q 9 4 2

East
- ♠ A J 9 7 3
- ♥ Q 7 4
- ♦ K 8 7 5
- ♣ 5

Me
- ♠ —
- ♥ A J 10 8 6 2
- ♦ A J 10 9 4 3
- ♣ 8

This was the first hand of the final quarter of the 1991 Vanderbilt final in Atlantic City. I won the club ace, played to the diamond ace, and ruffed a diamond. Now what? It looked as if I needed either to bring in the hearts for no losers, or to find diamonds 3-3. The percentage play seemed to be to play the heart king and, if the queen did not fall, ruff something to hand and lead a diamond, still surviving if West started with doubletons in both red suits.

All this was being watched on Vugraph, and everyone could see that if I just ruffed a club at trick four, I would gain the information that would lead me to the winning line, i.e., finessing the heart.

This was also the correct 'at the table' line. Why? Because West had thought for an hour over 6♥, obviously considering a sacrifice; therefore, heart shortness was very likely. Instead of using his huddle, I blocked it out, unwilling to finesse through the 4♠ bidder. And the lead made me feel that diamonds were almost certainly 4-2, since West might have led a diamond with ♦KQx. Anyway, if he had the king-queen of both minors, a singleton heart became even more likely.

An interesting sidelight is that once East shows out on the second club, you *could* lead a diamond planning, if West follows, to ruff with the *king*. Then finesse the heart eight, West obviously being 5-0-3-5. Perhaps this would have been right if West had thought for *two* hours over 6♥.

Making this hand would not, by itself, have been enough to win the match; but I feel that the psychological difference would probably have been enough to swing it.

CHAPTER SIX

HODGE PODGE

This chapter is a collection of random material that didn't fit neatly anywhere else. There are some instructive hands, some humorous stories, and my thoughts on a number of aspects of bridge and the way we play it. Let's start off with some hands that illustrate differing approaches to selecting a line of play by declarer.

POTPOURRI

Some hands do not lend themselves to 'normal' analysis. Sometimes you just have to look for a likely road to success without considering probability or technique. This example is from an IMPs-for-money game in New York, circa 1992:

Dummy

♠ 9 7
♥ A J 8 3
♦ A 6 5 2
♣ 10 8 3

Me

♠ A Q 10 8 3
♥ 6 5 2
♦ 4
♣ A J 5 2

WEST	NORTH	EAST	SOUTH
		1♦	1♠
pass	1NT	2♦	pass
pass	2♠	all pass	

West led the diamond ten. As I went through the various 'normal' lines in my head, nothing satisfied me. After a minute, I hit upon a method of enlisting the opposition's help. I ducked the first diamond and won the second, pitching a *club*. Then I passed the spade seven. West won the jack and duly switched to a club. It was now a simple matter to cross to the ace of hearts, pick up the spades, and set up my eighth trick in clubs.

The East hand:

♠ K 2   ♥ K 9   ♦ K Q J 8 7 3   ♣ K 9 4

Now, I'm not saying that no other line could lead to success, but I do believe that no other line is as likely to work, even against good opposition. Even if East gives suit-preference at trick two, how does he know what he wants? How will West figure out a subtle signal? It certainly won't be easy.

The only thing against me was the time it took me to find the play. Probably, it would be winning bridge to begin every hand you declare by looking for a line such as this — one which is just going to work — before thinking about the best technical play.

A definite weakness of mine is the desire I have to demonstrate to myself that I know what is happening. This occasionally causes me to make 'nullo' plays:

Dummy
- ♠ Q 10 7 5 2
- ♥ K 10
- ♦ J 9 6 5
- ♣ 7 4

Me
- ♠ 9
- ♥ A Q 6 3
- ♦ Q 10 7 3
- ♣ K 10 8 5

	N	
W		E
	S	

NORTH	SOUTH
	2NT
3♥[1]	4♣
4♥[2]	4♠
pass	

1. Transfer
2. Re-transfer

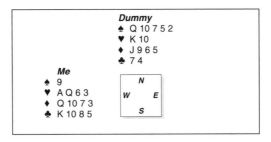

Trick 1: ♠9, ♠<u>10</u>, ♠3, ♠8

Trick 2: ♣4, ♣6, ♣Q, ♣<u>K</u>

Trick 3: ♥<u>A</u>, ♥10, ♥9, ♥4

Trick 4: ♥3, ♥<u>K</u>,♥ 2, ♥5

Trick 5: ♠2, ♠4, ♠<u>J</u>, ?

The obvious pitch was a heart, since partner's carding suggested that that would be safe. However, I satisfied myself, after some thought, that my fourth diamond could have no relevance. Therefore, in accordance with my desire to be different, I pitched a diamond. Declarer cashed the diamond ace, ruffed the jack of hearts in dummy (with me, typically, not covering), and led a diamond. As my partner thought on this trick I realized what I had perpetrated. Do you see it? Declarer's hand was obviously:

♠ A J 8　♥ J 5 4　♦ A K x x　♣ A Q J

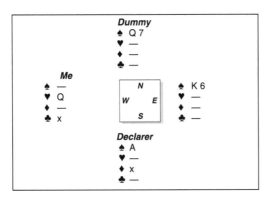

Partner had to pitch on this trick, and then declarer would cash the clubs and exit with a diamond. I would be on lead in a two-card ending (see left), forced to smother my partner's king of spades. I had never seen a smother play at the table before, and have never believed any report I ever read of one. Fortunately(?) for me, declarer, who was not 'into the hand', cashed the spade ace and conceded down one.

Accurate handling of suit-combinations sometimes requires intricate analysis:

Dummy

♠ A 6
♥ K 4 3 2
♦ K Q 6
♣ A K 7 3

```
        N
    W       E
        S
```

You

♠ 8 5 3 2
♥ A 10 9 7 5
♦ A 4
♣ J 6

Matchpoints

WEST	NORTH	EAST	SOUTH
	1♣	pass	1♥
2♠	3♠	pass	4♦
pass	4♥	all pass	

West leads the spade king. Think before reading on.

Dummy

♠ A 6
♥ K 4 3 2
♦ K Q 6
♣ A K 7 3

You

♠ 8 5 3 2
♥ A 10 9 7 5
♦ A 4
♣ J 6

The contract is clearly in no danger — the major issue is five or six. The only complication is that 4-0 trumps puts five in jeopardy. The solution is to cross to the diamond ace and lead the *ten* of hearts. If West follows, go up with the king and continue normally, but if West shows out *you must duck*. Win the return, finesse the heart seven, and concede a spade. Later, ruff a spade with the heart king, finesse the heart nine, and pitch the other spade on the diamond. Five made — the only way it *should* be made.

I must admit to altering this hand. It was originally presented to me by my wife, Debbie, with the spade ace in South's hand, and with South's hearts being ♥A10987. This meant that declarer, winning the opening lead and playing a 'small' heart, could 'fall into' the correct line. With my alteration, the winning play will be found only by someone who knows *why*.

Sometimes the reason a hand *should* be made is far from obvious, even at double-dummy. The following hand played by Zia in a National pairs game is a case in point:

Dummy
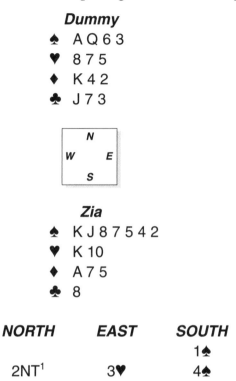
♠ A Q 6 3
♥ 8 7 5
♦ K 4 2
♣ J 7 3

Zia
♠ K J 8 7 5 4 2
♥ K 10
♦ A 7 5
♣ 8

WEST	NORTH	EAST	SOUTH
			1♠
dbl	2NT[1]	3♥	4♠
all pass			

1. Limit raise

West led the ace of clubs and continued with the king, East playing the five and then the six (low-high discouraging). Zia ruffed, and immediately led a diamond, hoping that West would fail to unblock. West, however, played the jack; so Zia drew trumps (West had both missing trumps), eliminated clubs, and exited in diamonds — in the forlorn hope that West had started with ♦QJ10 alone, or any five.

These were the four hands:

Dummy

♠ A Q 6 3
♥ 8 7 5
♦ K 4 2
♣ J 7 3

```
        N
♠ 10 9         ♠ —
♥ A 6 3 2  W   E  ♥ Q J 9 4
♦ J 10         ♦ Q 9 8 6 3
♣ A K Q 4 2    S  ♣ 10 9 6 5
```

Zia

♠ K J 8 7 5 4 2
♥ K 10
♦ A 7 5
♣ 8

Obviously, the hand could have been made by throwing West in with a club, but I sympathized with Zia since it seemed unnatural to play the takeout doubler for a doubleton diamond. It was only later, when I looked at the hand record, that I realized the significance of the spot cards.

If East had the club queen, he would surely encourage with his highest spot. Therefore, East did not hold the club queen. That being the case, East was likely to have four clubs, not only because he might have discouraged with a lower spot, but also because most people do not usually go around playing middle cards from five small. Now that West is known to have five clubs, and subsequently shows up with two spades, he is quite likely to have two diamonds. And thus (as usual?), the winning line is the logical one.

Suit-combinations

It sometimes seems to me that the most important rule for defenders in handling suit-combinations is

Always play the nine unless you must

For example:

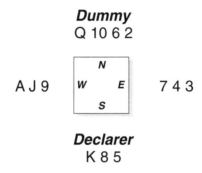

Dummy
Q 10 6 2

A J 9

7 4 3

Declarer
K 8 5

When declarer leads low, West must play the jack to give the defense a chance for two tricks.

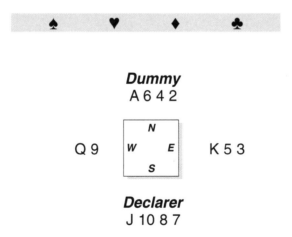

Dummy
A 6 4 2

Q 9

K 5 3

Declarer
J 10 8 7

When declarer leads the ten, West needs to play the queen

smoothly, and South should go wrong. This may look risky
— what if declarer has the king? Well, if a six-card suit in
the hidden hand is possible, the risk is very real (bare king);
but, if not, then it is probable that, either declarer doesn't
have the king, or that he is intending to finesse through you
anyway. It is unlikely that the ten will be played to the ace,
since you may hold Q9xx. Yes, I know game theory is
involved here, but most players simply aren't willing to
look that foolish. Certainly, if declarer were known to hold
only four, I would deem the risk infinitesimal.

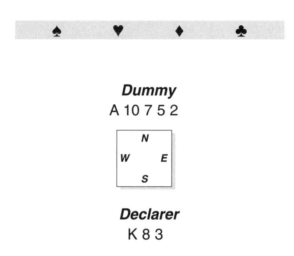

Dummy
A 10 7 5 2

Declarer
K 8 3

The problem here is to take four tricks while keeping East
off lead. Attempting to lead to the eight will fail if East has
J9x and inserts the nine, West unblocking the queen. The
answer is to lead towards the ace, ducking if West plays the
queen. If not, duck the nine on the way back.

Dummy
A K 10 8 x

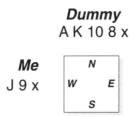

Me
J 9 x

Declarer in three notrump, with plenty of entries, led towards dummy in this suit, in which he was known to have fewer than three cards. This was an exception to the 'nine' rule. Instinctively, I played the jack and declarer, who started with a singleton, misguessed and played me for QJx. Probably, he should have guessed right, but at least I had given him a chance to go wrong.

Dummy
A 2

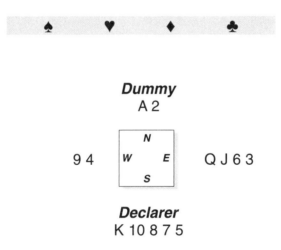

9 4   Q J 6 3

Declarer
K 10 8 7 5

When dummy plays the ace, you must play the nine. Here, declarer should still guess right in theory, but in practice will likely play you for J9 or Q9.

Those were all pretty old hat, but here is a little-known wrinkle:

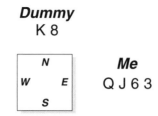

Dummy
K 8

Me
Q J 6 3

This position arose in the 1995 Macallan Pairs, and I was East. Declarer was known to have ace-fifth in this suit and, fortunately, he took a long time at trick one, so I was able to figure out this position at the table.

Clearly, I did not want to split if declarer had A109xx or A97xx and, also clearly, partner needed to play the nine from 9x. But, if partner played the nine from 97 and I didn't split, this would be a disaster, since declarer would have no choice but to stick in the ten. Similarly, if partner played the seven from 7x and I *did* split, that wouldn't be too good either. Therefore, partner must only play the seven from 97 or 107, the nine from 9x (not 97), and the x from 7x.

I found it staggering that there could exist such a combination where it was fatal to play the seven from 7x. In fact, if you switch the six and the seven, you will see that the same thing is true of 6x.

Dummy

A 5 2

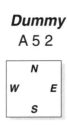

Declarer

K 10 8 7 6

This combination is not well-known, even though it appeared in *The Bridge World*. The correct technical play for four tricks is to lead low from the ace, intending to play low. If East plays an honor you can claim four tricks (except on a 5-0 break, when there is no chance anyway). If East plays the nine, insert the ten — this loses only to singleton nine in either hand. As a practical matter, you may want to go up king when East plays the nine. Would *you* know to play the nine from QJ9x? You should, if you just follow the golden rule.

Here is an interesting and little-known combination:

Dummy

Q J 8 3

Declarer

A 9 4

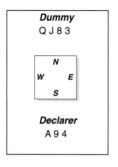

Dummy
Q J 8 3

Declarer
A 9 4

The contract is notrump, you need three tricks, and dummy has no entry. How would you proceed? Analysis shows that the best play is low to the eight, planning to run the queen if the eight wins, and to cash the ace if East wins the ten. This succeeds (apparently) whenever West has the ten and East has the king, or whenever the king is doubleton. But this is not so — East can *duck* with 10xxx! (Also, West can play the 10 with K10-doubleton.) Steve Sion claims to have ducked with ten-fourth at the table. I find this a little difficult to believe (probably envy), but I'm impressed that he even thought of it.

Debbie and I were going over some hands from a regional in Rye, New York, in which she had played in 1998, and we came upon the following:

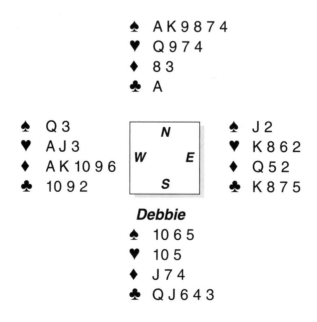

♠ A K 9 8 7 4
♥ Q 9 7 4
♦ 8 3
♣ A

♠ Q 3
♥ A J 3
♦ A K 10 9 6
♣ 10 9 2

♠ J 2
♥ K 8 6 2
♦ Q 5 2
♣ K 8 7 5

Debbie
♠ 10 6 5
♥ 10 5
♦ J 7 4
♣ Q J 6 4 3

"What happened on this board?" I asked.

"Nothing — boring hand," answered Debbie. "We didn't compete to 3♠ over 3♦."

"Would you have made 3♠? No, I guess not. The eight of hearts stands up."

"Okay, next hand," said Debbie.

"Wait a minute," I mused. "The defense leads three rounds of diamonds, and declarer ruffs and draws trumps. What if you now lead a heart to the five? West is forced to win the jack, and now you make a heart trick by force."

"Did I say this hand was boring?" said Debbie, smiling.

"But wait, if East puts in the six he foils the declarer. Now the eight comes back into play."

"I guess this is a bad hand for upside-down," Debbie remarked.

Thinking more about this combination the next day, I realized the flaw of a heart to the five. Declarer would be relinquishing the legitimate chance of West's having the ♥A8x or ♥K8x. After playing small to the ten, declarer could eventually pin the eight.

However, this thought brought about another point of interest. If the ten loses to the ♥A or ♥K, declarer can apparently play the ♥Q or ♥9 with the same effect. Not so! If declarer plays the ♥Q and it goes ♥K, ♥5, ♥8, she would now need to guess whether West started with ♥AJ8 or ♥A8x. No, declarer must play the nine on the second round, to discover the whereabouts of the jack. If West played the ace from ♥AJx, that was a Grosvenor.

My thoughts on this hand give you an idea of how my (strange) mind works.

FALSECARDING

Not much has been written on this subject — perhaps because it is too random. I would like to deal with one particular aspect: which card should declarer play from equals?

Many of the basic rules are well-known, but it really surprises me how often expert declarers hurt themselves by violating simple precepts. For example, if RHO leads through you, and you don't play your highest from equals, RHO will 'know' that you have the other equal (since his partner failed to win the trick with it). Obviously, there may be occasions when one is only (or primarily) involved with LHO, but I have seen experts make life easy for their opponents time and again with this type of error.

Another common error occurs when LHO leads, dummy has nothing relevant, and RHO wins the trick; usually, you should not drop the highest from equals, as this often gives maximum information to the opposition. With three touching cards it is frequently correct to play the *middle* one as in the following layout:

Dummy
K 9 6 3

```
    N
W       E
    S
```

Declarer
Q J 10

West leads the deuce in a suit contract, and East wins the ace. You happen to know that the lead is a singleton (either from the bidding or from the opponents' carding methods).

If you play the queen or the ten, East will know also, as the lead could not be from QJ2 or J102. But if you play the *jack*, you can keep an element of doubt in East's mind — Q102 is possible.

Of course, there are times when you *want* to give the opponents information. A well-known piece of chicanery is, when playing notrump, to win the opening lead with the queen from king-queen doubleton facing two or three small. LHO knows that you have the king and may, therefore, shift upon gaining the lead. Of course, your opponent may wonder why you are being so generous, and figure out to lay down the ace.

That brings to mind a more subtle form of trickery — winning the queen from king-queen-third. Now, LHO might decide to bang down that ace and drop your *deuce* — it all depends upon the opponents.

Some falsecards are mandatory. In other situations, it is important that you falsecard frequently and randomly, both as declarer and defender. Otherwise, you make yourself a little too easy to play against.

BIDDING SYSTEM AND STYLE

I believe that Bob Hamman once said, "System is 3% of the game." (I once asked him if he really said it, and he answered, "Why so much?")

I have no idea how true this statement is, but I feel more or less the same way. However, I would put it a little differently. I would say that the choice of basic system, conventions and gadgets is relatively unimportant. I do regard *agreements* as being of primary importance. The more situations in which you and your partner are attuned to the same wavelength, the better equipped you will be to handle different possibilities. To do this requires definition more than artificiality.

Take Key Card Blackwood (Edgar Kaplan would have said, "Please."). In the hands of the perfect partnership, I believe this can be a useful, well-nigh invaluable tool. However, unless you are prepared to spend many hours discussing the various problems involved, you're probably better off without it, since it is extremely accident-prone.

I feel that the proliferation of conventions nowadays is not good for the game — for a couple of reasons. Firstly, I believe that it makes the game less marketable in terms of attracting both new players and media coverage. Secondly, I think that so much artificiality makes it difficult to develop the good (conventional?!) judgment that stems from natural bidding.

As for bidding style, arguments rage as to who is 'right'. Sound or light openings? Light or solid preempts? Four- or five-card majors? Limit or forcing style? Weak or strong notrump? And on, and on. Can it be that one group of experts is correct in these arguments, and the other just plain wrong?

I believe that the important thing is for each player to play the style which creates the most comfort for his own partnership. This is most likely to produce the best decisions in judgment and card-play.

I have not had much to say about bidding because I feel that talking about the subject is analogous to talking about religion. One can talk and argue and talk and argue, but neither side will be persuaded to change, except perhaps on rare occasions.

There is, however, one aspect of bidding which I believe it is necessary to master if one is to be a true expert: *playing the hand during the bidding.*

This is most commonly applied in slam-bidding. Except for quantitatively bid slams (which occur when one partner has bid notrump), you should invariably 'play' the slam before bidding it. That is to say, you give partner the hand or hands you think are most consistent with the bidding to date, and check to be sure that slam is good on balance.

This principle can be extended to the game level. Whenever one of your choices involves a final decision, try giving partner three hands: the best hand he might have, the worst hand, and an average hand (I learned this from Zia). This should give you a good idea of whether to accept, invite, or pass.

Applying this technique will sometimes lead to a contract that might not otherwise have been considered, e.g., you hold:

♠ K J 8 5 3   ♥ K 4   ♦ A K   ♣ J 10 9 4

Partner opens 2♠ (weak — but sound), and RHO overcalls 3♥. Many players would bid 4♠ without thought; but give partner a normal hand and you see that three notrump is worthy of consideration, if not completely clear-cut.

Furthermore, 'playing' the hand in this way will improve your declarer play, since you will be more focused in general, and more prepared in particular, on each hand you declare.

PSYCHIC BIDDING

Can psyching be a percentage action? Should it even be legal within the game of bridge? I would answer 'yes, probably' to the first question, and a resounding 'yes' to the second.

The question of whether psyching is advisable is almost purely subjective. Ira Rubin once told me, "I only psyche against players who are better than I am — I haven't psyched yet." However, there are certain situations where psyches are almost commonplace, for example, over takeout doubles or game tries. The most successful psyches occur where the psycher is in total control of the auction, but is playing in a new partnership. Then partner will not know enough about the psycher's tendencies to alert the opponents.

True experts are aware of situations where their opponent has a 'free' psyche, and will think accordingly. I believe that, if the overall level of play were higher, there would be more reason for a deep analysis of the subject. The way everyone plays right now, all you need to do to win, even against the world's best, is to play sound bridge.

Once upon a time, I dabbled in psyches — mostly at rubber bridge where I felt less responsibility to my partner. Later in my career I conceived the idea of psyching a strong notrump in first seat at favorable vulnerability. The conditions I preferred were IMPs scoring, with the opponents playing a double as some sort of artificial bid. I presumed that any hand valued below 15-17 would be opened 1NT, regardless of distribution. I analyzed hundreds of hands using this scenario, and the psyche scored a huge net profit. The analysis uncovered occasional disasters (I never exposed the psyche by passing a forcing bid, and I assumed that partner *never* 'read' the psyche), and many small losses (down four or five against a part-score was not uncommon); but these were more than counterbalanced by frequent game swings, either because the opponents were talked out of their game (slam?), or because a no-play game was allowed to make due to confusion. The ideal situation was for each opponent to hold a balanced opening bid or better, and for them to defend one notrump or three notrump while they were cold for three notrump (or slam!). Even if they came into the bidding, analysis showed that it would be difficult for them to achieve a par result. Indeed, some partnerships have an agreement that they 'never' bid game against a strong notrump.

I experimented a couple of times with mixed success. Then I decided to back my judgment and, in the finals of the 1992 World Championship in Salsamaggiore, I opened 1NT with a balanced seven-count. The result? My partner, Seymon Deutsch, raised to 3NT with 10 points. Vugraph commentators were certain that there was some reporting error, since I was considered a 'straight' player. Only Debbie, who was in the audience, knew the truth.

The opponents' defense was understandably poor, and I emerged with eight tricks. In the other room, my teammates also took eight tricks in notrump for +120 and a gain of 2 IMPs. I remember that Hamman told me I was crazy, and maybe he was right, but it was great theater and, I then believed, winning bridge.

Subsequent to that time, analysis of more hands produced less favorable results for the psyche, so I scrapped the idea. I never had a chance to make this psyche with Zia because we play a weak notrump non-vulnerable.

Probably, I'll never get involved in something like that again.

THE LAWS

I have never felt comfortable with enforcing the 'letter of the law' as regards revokes, leads and calls out of turn, and penalty cards. Zia and I do not allow ourselves to profit from mechanical errors. Assuming that we feel we have not been damaged by the potential unauthorized information, we prefer to let our opponents take them back. (I do not in any way expect my opponents to do the same if I commit such an infraction. I *would* retract my error if my opponent asked me to do so, but I would never suggest it myself.)

I think that the rules ought to be that the penalties for mechanical infractions are not automatic, but adjudicated on a case-by-case basis. Leading out of the wrong hand, for which (strangely) there is no penalty, should be subject to the same standards. "But," you might object, "all this could lead to more complications." It might, but I feel that it would be a more equitable rule and, after all, these infractions do not occur all that frequently. The only problem I can foresee is the possibility that the 'laxer' rules might lead to more revokes, etc., but I do not think that likely. (And we can cross that bridge when we come to it.)

As lenient as I am about revokes, I am strict about claims and concessions. The rules are stringent here, as I believe they should be. The player who claims, unlike one who revokes, is consciously attempting to get what he believes he is entitled to (at least I assume so), *and will frequently get an incorrect concession from the opponents*. To counterbalance this, false claims, when caught, should be penalized to the fullest possible extent.

A simple example: declarer in a grand slam has a trump suit of AKxx in dummy and J10xxxx in hand. After winning a side-suit opening lead, declarer claims. Clearly, he makes if trumps are 2-1 and goes down if RHO has Qxx.

But what if LHO has Qxx? Declarer would 'obviously' make on the marked finesse, assuming a return to hand would not be ruffed or overruffed. But, the ruling should be *down one*. Why?

Because the basis for declarer's claim might have been simply that he thought he had eleven trumps and would, therefore, have just cashed the other high trump.

THE 'LAW'

The following article was written tongue-in-cheek at about the same time as Larry's book, *To Bid or Not to Bid*, was published. I thought my article could lead to an entertaining discourse about the 'Law of Total Tricks', but Larry surprised me by preferring that I not publish it. So I didn't — until now. Sorry, Larry.

I do believe that the 'Law' is a valuable tool but, at least for an expert, it should be an extension to (not a replacement for) good bidding judgment.

LARRY COHEN IN NETHERLAND

He looked around feeling dizzy. Suddenly he noticed a small figure with a red face and little horns, seated at a desk.

"You are Larry Cohen, the bridge player from Florida," said the little devil, more for the benefit of the reader than for any other reason...

"Yes," said Larry, although he realized he was being spoken to informatively, not interrogatively.

"Welcome," said the figure.

"Wait a minute," said Larry, glancing around and noticing the generally fiery surroundings. "There must be some mistake. I'm in the wrong place. I didn't even know I was dead! I lived a good life, I shouldn't be here. I never intentionally broke the law."

"Making bad laws is no better than breaking good ones."

"Is that it? But I was right, I'm sure of it. You must give me a chance to prove the Law's validity."

In the twinkling of an eye, Larry found himself in another room seated at a card table with three females dressed all in black. "Which... I mean, who are you?" asked Larry.

"We're the Brew Team."

Larry suddenly discovered he was holding cards. He looked and saw:

♠ A K 9 8 5   ♥ 9 8 6 5   ♦ 8   ♣ 8 5 4

The bidding, without the use of boxes, proceeded:

Witch 1 WEST	Witch 2 NORTH	Witch 3 EAST	Larry SOUTH
		2♦	pass
2NT	pass	3♦	pass
pass	dbl	pass	3♠
4♦	pass	pass	?

"What's the vulnerability?" asked Larry.

"Shut up and bid," said Witch No. 3, rather illogically.

Apparently, he would have to make a decision without further information. What did the Law say? Well, there were probably at least nineteen combined trumps on average, and twenty was far from unlikely. There also might be a double fit if Witch No. 2 had good hearts. Therefore, bidding seemed indicated. Larry bid 4♥ to be flexible, and his partner corrected to 4♠. West led the club king, and dummy produced:

♠ Q 10 7 3   ♥ A K Q   ♦ 7 4   ♣ Q J 10 3

East signaled with the nine and the defense took the first four tricks. Well, thought Larry, if spades are 3-1 and hearts break 4-2 (i.e., if East is 1-4-6-2 or 3-2-6-2), then the Law works perfectly, since 4♦ makes. This was the full deal:

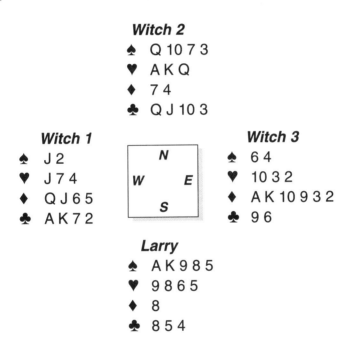

Witch 2
♠ Q 10 7 3
♥ A K Q
♦ 7 4
♣ Q J 10 3

Witch 1
♠ J 2
♥ J 7 4
♦ Q J 6 5
♣ A K 7 2

Witch 3
♠ 6 4
♥ 10 3 2
♦ A K 10 9 3 2
♣ 9 6

Larry
♠ A K 9 8 5
♥ 9 8 6 5
♦ 8
♣ 8 5 4

"Nineteen trumps! Seventeen tricks!" screeched the witches in unison.

"But... ," began Larry.

"Shut up," said Witch No. 3.

Larry discovered that he was holding cards again. He looked and saw that he had exactly the same hand he'd just held. To the surprise of no one, (including you), the bidding proceeded exactly as it had before. Larry was clear-headed enough to realize that, if he changed his bid, they would change the deal. So he bid 4♥ again, and there followed an exact repetition of the events above, except that this time West doubled.

"You don't learn from your mistakes, do you?" sneered Witch No.1.

"But why did you double this time?" asked Larry.

"Because I do," answered Witch No. 1.

For the third time, Larry was looking at his 5-4-1-3 seven-count and, for the third time, 4♦ came round to him. By now, he figured that there was no escaping his destiny. Anyway, maybe it *was* wrong to bid. Partner had pushed the opponents, and there was no real double fit. So, he passed and led the spade king. This was the full deal:

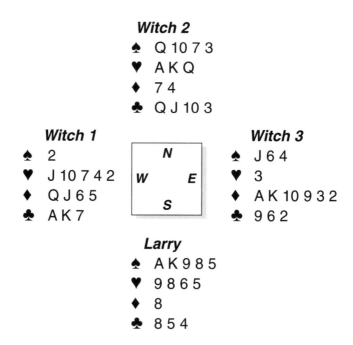

Witch 2
♠ Q 10 7 3
♥ A K Q
♦ 7 4
♣ Q J 10 3

Witch 1
♠ 2
♥ J 10 7 4 2
♦ Q J 6 5
♣ A K 7

Witch 3
♠ J 6 4
♥ 3
♦ A K 10 9 3 2
♣ 9 6 2

Larry
♠ A K 9 8 5
♥ 9 8 6 5
♦ 8
♣ 8 5 4

Due to the heart position, even a club lead could not prevent eleven tricks in diamonds. Also, of course, 4♠ was cold.

"Nineteen trumps! Twenty-one tricks!" screeched the witches.

"But... ," began Larry.

"Shut up," said Witch No. 3, who appeared to have a limited vocabulary.

"Yes," said Witch No. 2, "with the same North-South hands there was a *four*-trick difference in the number of total tricks. You say it can always be off by one, but the truth is, it can be off by two or more with no valid explanation. Sound and logical judgment can be used in lieu of your Law, except at high levels where your Law does not work efficiently anyway. The only real use for your Law is in avoiding total aberrations."

Larry sighed. He knew there was no escape. All he could do was wait for the three words he needed to hear that would save him from his fate.

"Wake up, Larry."

MASTERPOINTS

Speaking as someone who doesn't have an abundance of them, I think masterpoints are a joke.

They cannot be used as a testament to a player's strength, but only to his or her longevity — a new system is needed. In this computerized age it should not be too difficult to set up a system similar to the 'Elo' ranking in chess. The significant factors are importance of event, timeliness of event, strength of opponents, strength of partner (and teammates), and result. This would give players a current ranking that would have some actual relevance.

The old system can still be maintained for those who want it.

WOMEN'S BRIDGE

There is rampant sexism in bridge. Women are generally regarded as inferior to men as bridge players. Almost all players (male and female) would feel more confident playing against a woman whom they have never seen before than they would against a man. In mixed pairs, many players plan strategies and make choices based purely on the sex of a particular opponent. Why is this?

I believe that there is basically no reason why a player's sex should define his or her ability. My reasoning is this: I look at all the world's best players and see no common characteristic. There are aggressives, conservatives, analyticals, instinctuals, bashers, scientists, toughies, easies, etc. If there *is* a fundamental difference between the sexes as regards brain power, I do not see any logic in extending that to the game of bridge.

Why is it then that if you asked the most highly regarded players in the world to list their top twenty players, none of them would name a woman? (I could probably have safely picked a higher number.)

One major factor is women's bridge. At one time, almost all competitive players were men. When more females entered the game, instead of competing against the best they frequently played among themselves. The best way to improve is to compete against better players. Just think of all the women's events that have been held in the last thirty years. Now imagine that all of those females had, instead, competed in an open forum. Once all the players were assimilated, is it not likely that some of the current world's best would be female?

Another factor is perception. Imagine that a female today *were* actually one of the world's top ten players. Are you certain that anyone would know it? It is extremely difficult to compare the individual talent of bridge players;

but it seems to be easy for people to look at an open team containing a female and say, "They won *even with a woman*." Or (after they lost), "They had *a woman* on their team." This sort of attitude can become self-realizing.

When players are considering prospective partners or teammates, I believe gender is a factor — some people will simply *never* want to play with a female, nor want one on their team. A male can be insulted by saying that he 'plays like a girl.' A female can be 'complimented' by saying that she 'plays well for a woman.' The simple phrase (commonly used) 'woman bridge player' is a negative classification. People will call a female a 'top woman bridge player' or 'one of the best woman players in the world,' without having any idea that it could be anything other than a high compliment.

In case you haven't guessed it yet, I am against women's bridge. While it might be nice to win a world championship, or to be hired to play professionally, I don't believe there is any more justification for separating people in this way than in having tournaments for, say, people with brown hair, with big noses, or weighing over 200 lb. Probably, if someone were to bring a lawsuit against the ACBL, it would be the end of women's events.

I guess there could be an 'A' and a 'B' event if there were a demand for it. But, the current method hinders women's ability to improve the quality of their play. Yes, they have a choice, but the lure of women's bridge with its championships and financial opportunity is naturally irresistible to most of the country's top female players.

Of course, I realize that it would be unpopular and impractical to terminate women's bridge. Obviously, these events produce a substantial amount of revenue for the various organizing bodies. Therefore, all I can do is recommend that females who are serious about being the best they can be shun them and compete only in open events.

JUNIOR BRIDGE

Just in case my views on women's bridge lead you to believe that I am against everything other than totally open bridge, let me correct that impression. I wholeheartedly approve of events constructed for junior players. I'm not sure exactly how to justify this. It just feels 'right' to me — just as women's bridge feels 'wrong'. I think it is good that young players experience the excitement and pressure of competing for (say) a world championship. Also, it highlights, for everyone to see, some of the stars of tomorrow. I'm less sure about seniors' bridge, but I guess I don't see that it is doing any harm.

PROFESSIONAL BRIDGE

I don't have much to say on this subject. Obviously, the game would be 'purer' if there were no professionalism or money involved, but there would also be less incentive. Many players would not be able to devote the time they do to studying and playing the game if they did not play professionally. The only way out of the current client-professional situation would be through...

SPONSORSHIP

There is some sponsorship in bridge, but not much. Of course, I'm now talking about sponsors who do not intend to compete themselves. How can we hope to attract widespread sponsorship? As things now stand we have no chance. Bridge is not marketable because the basics are complicated. If a non-player were to turn on the TV and watch bridge, he or she would not be able to understand what was happening. And even those who know the rules would be mystified watching most modern expert competition, due to the phenomenal amount of artificiality that exists today. Perhaps it would be beneficial for the future promotion of the game if the authorities clamped down and enforced some type of unified or universal system.

SYSTEMS

I know many people would be horrified by the idea of a universal system, but it would not bother me. Personally, I think bridge is more enjoyable when the game revolves around bidding judgment and card-play, rather than systemic understanding (especially *destructive* systemic understanding). I would prefer that any convention which currently requires a prepared written defense be made illegal. This would simplify the game. The booklets prepared by the ACBL and WBF are good, but the whole idea is contrived. Let's attack the disease rather than the symptom — that's the way I see it.

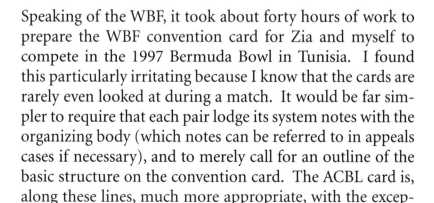

Speaking of the WBF, it took about forty hours of work to prepare the WBF convention card for Zia and myself to compete in the 1997 Bermuda Bowl in Tunisia. I found this particularly irritating because I know that the cards are rarely even looked at during a match. It would be far simpler to require that each pair lodge its system notes with the organizing body (which notes can be referred to in appeals cases if necessary), and to merely call for an outline of the basic structure on the convention card. The ACBL card is, along these lines, much more appropriate, with the exception that there should be a separate card comprehensively defining all carding agreements. (This is important information which is often hidden.)

SPECIAL CONTESTS

Bridge in the form of bidding contests is not real bridge. Magazines usually have bidding contests such as *The Bridge World*'s 'Challenge the Champs'. I am sorry to have to reveal this (actually, that's a lie — I'm not in the least bit sorry), but the whole thing is really a sham. The players who participate in these contests are often not monitored and, even when they are, they are permitted to retract and change bids. Since the hands are not randomly selected (in fact, they are often submitted with emphasis on a particular facet), one should not bid the same way as one would in real bridge. Here are a few 'rules' which I have compiled for bidding contests:

1) *Whenever you hold Qx, count it as 0 HCP, except when partner bids the suit naturally (then count it as 4 HCP).*

2) *Whenever you have game values and an 8-card major fit:*
   a) *With flat shape, stop in a partial.*
   b) *With distribution, play slam or 3NT.*

3) *In every set, look for the combined 27+ HCP hand that does not produce game.*

4) *In every set, look for the 4-3 fit that makes a grand (with the 'better' fit having no play).*

5) *Never open 2NT.*

6) *On competitive hands, always have 'pure' values.*

7) *Passing the hand out can never yield the top score.*

All this does not mean that it is useless to bid these hands for practice. It's only useless if you care about your score.

Contests which involve card-play are another kettle of fish. Double-dummy hands, for example, can be fascinating, and can even be educational, since they often show you what the cards *can* do. While the problems and solutions are often too unrealistic for practical application, situations do arise, usually after a competitive auction, where both declarer and defender(s) are playing double-dummy, or close to it. Working on double-dummy problems can sharpen your ability to imagine unusual possibilities.

A close relative of the double-dummy problem is the play-or-defend problem. I was interested when I noticed a pattern — always play, never defend. I think the reason is that declarer, who has more assets (usually several more), has more weapons. No matter what the defense can do, he usually has another string to his bow. Early in 1998, Phil Martin gave me this play-or-defend problem[1]:

---

1. I asked Phil for the source of the hand, and he told me that he had seen it in an article by Eddie Kantar in a 1955 copy of *The Bridge World*.

Dummy

♠ 7 6 3
♥ J 8
♦ A K Q 6 5
♣ 10 7 3

♠ Q J 9
♥ 6 4
♦ J 10 8 7
♣ Q 8 6 4

```
      N
 W        E
      S
```

♠ K 10 8 5 4
♥ 9 5 2
♦ 9 4
♣ K 9 5

Declarer

♠ A 2
♥ A K Q 10 7 3
♦ 3 2
♣ A J 2

"You and your friend walk into a rubber bridge club and kibitz a ten-cent game that is just starting up," Phil began. "You both watch North-South bid to 6♥, and West leads the spade queen. Just as dummy is being tabled, both South and West get urgent telephone calls and need to leave the club. You and your friend are asked to fill in. Your friend offers you the choice of sitting South or West. What do you do?"

"Now that you've finished your silly preamble, do you mind if I work on the problem," I replied caustically.

Since there was no clear route to twelve tricks, it was obvious to me from the start that it had to be right to be declarer. I could see there was only one chance — a squeeze against West. Ducking the lead didn't seem right, so I tried winning the first spade and running trumps. West could throw a club and a spade, but on the fifth heart he would need to throw his last spade, in order to hold three clubs. Dummy pitches two spades and a diamond.

Now on the last trump West must pitch a club, and dummy pitches a diamond. Now I can cross to a diamond and lead the club ten, making two club tricks while keeping East off lead (if East covers, win and play a low club). Too easy. What's the problem?

Then I spotted the flaw. On the fifth trump West did not need to pitch his last spade — he could pitch a club safely. If I led a low club the defense could cash a spade, and if I took my pitch I couldn't force a second club trick. I went over and over it, but couldn't make any headway.

I retraced my steps and tried ducking the first spade. Winning the second spade, I ran trumps. After five rounds West would have to come down to a stiff club. If he instead pitched his last spade, the sixth trump would force him to unguard clubs. Now the run of the diamonds would squeeze East in the black suits. After West is reduced to stiffs in the blacks, the sixth trump finishes him. If he pitches a spade East will be squeezed, and if he pitches the club queen I can take a finesse. In other words, a guard squeeze. What's wrong with that?

Well, West didn't need to continue spades at trick two. A club switch would break up the guard squeeze, and West would obviously switch to the queen of clubs to avoid being squeezed in the minors. After that, declarer was clearly dead.

I worked on the problem a little longer, because this did not seem intricate enough to justify Phil's giving me this problem. Eventually, I conceded and went to talk to Phil.

"I give up," I told him. "I know it's right to play but I can't figure out how to make it."

"So you choose to defend?" asked Phil with a sneaky smile.

"Not willingly, but yes," I said.

"At ten cents a point?" asked Phil a little too eagerly.

"No way," I stated. "The jack of spades ain't gonna

squirt no cider in *my* ear."

"Pretend, then," said Phil.

"Okay. I defend."

"I duck the opening lead," said Phil.

"I shift to the club queen," I countered.

"You owe me five dollars," said Phil.

"Why? You're minus."

"I may be down, but I'm not minus. Remember the form of scoring? I have 100 honors!"

Maybe that preamble wasn't so silly, after all.

Par contests, while apparently more true to real bridge, suffer from the same flaw as bidding contests — non-random selection. In a way, it is even worse, because you know there is an answer at which you can logically arrive. Having said that, I must admit that I love par hands and hope one day to participate in a par contest.* One of the reasons I sometimes take too much time at the table is that I'm looking for the 'answer' — but none exists.

Bidding problems presented to a panel, such as *The Bridge World*'s 'Master Solvers' Club', are entertaining and educational. I have learned much from reading the experts' comments. I would like to see more of 'giving the other hand' as a problem a few months later (or the same hand a few years later). Often, in presenting the comments by the

---

*After this book was completed, I did actually compete in the Jean Besse Par Contest at the 1998 World Championships in Lille, France. I won the gold medal. I have also written a series of articles about the contest for BRIDGE TODAY magazine.

same players at a later date, an expert is exposed as being full of nonsense. In fact, until we can 'clone' human beings, we will never discover the 'truth'.

Imagine a team of four Al Roths against a team of four Ira Rubins. Perhaps we would finally discover who (if anyone) is full of it.

HUMOR

Before entering the driest chapter of the book (ethics), I would like to relate two stories which I find amusing.

The first took place at one of Edgar Kaplan's home IMP games. During the first match, Edgar's teammates allowed a game to be made because the opening leader, holding ♣KQJx, led his partner's suit instead. Edgar's comment was, "When God gives you the KQJ of a suit, he is telling you what to lead."

In the second match, Edgar was partnered by Brad Moss, who told me this story. The opponents were bidding towards slam, and Edgar doubled a 5♣ cuebid. They reached 6♥ and Brad (naturally) held ♦KQJx. He led a high diamond and the contract made, whereas a club lead would have defeated it. Brad was embarrassed and apologetic. "I should have led a club," he said.

"You shouldn't feel too bad." said Edgar comfortingly. "It was a guess. God told you to lead something, and I told you to lead something else. You guessed wrong, that's all."

The second story concerns a partnership of brothers, whom I shall call Bob and Jim. A long time ago, soon after they started playing, Jim noticed a disturbing trend. When he opened, say, 1♠, Bob, holding a nine or ten-count, would bid "TWO SPADES" in ringing tones. However, when he held a five or six-count he would bid "two spades" in a quiet voice.

"This has got to stop," Jim told his brother, when he explained the situation. "It's unethical."

"I promise it won't happen again," said Bob. "I'm sorry, I really wasn't aware I was doing it."

"If you do it again, I'll punish you," said Jim.

The next time they played together was a regional in New York, and Jim arrived barely on time. Bob and his opponents were waiting to play. On the first hand, Jim opened 1♠ and Bob bid "TWO SPADES" in a loud voice. Jim was very upset that Bob had ignored their conversation and vowed to teach him a lesson. He had a sound game try and passed, fully expecting to miss game and get a poor score. Bob tabled a five-count and eight tricks proved to be the limit of the hand. Jim was now almost apoplectic.

"That's the most despicable thing I've ever seen," he yelled. "How could you take advantage of our conversation like that? Have you no shame?"

He continued ranting in this vein until he was forced to breathe. Bob, who had sat stoically through his brother's whole tirade, turned calmly to the man on his right and said...

"Would you mind repeating what you said to me before my brother came to the table?"

"Oh, not at all," replied the man. "I told you that my wife is a little hard of hearing, so could you please raise your voice when you bid?"

CHAPTER SEVEN

ETHICS

WARNING

The following chapter is abstruse, and is likely to lead to extreme confusion and/or boredom. It should be skipped except by those interested in the purity of the game.

1992 REVISITED

I'd like to begin this chapter by reprinting an article I wrote for *Bridge Today* in early 1992. It has been slightly altered for inclusion in this book, in order to spare my editor any feelings of nausea arising from my grammar, syntax and punctuation.

ETHICS FOR ADVANCED PLAYERS

How important are ethics to the game of bridge? To my mind they are crucial. If the foundation of bridge is not completely 'clean', then the entire game is tainted.

The sad truth is that every player is guilty of some ethical misdemeanors, i.e., those of which the player is unaware (when he *is* aware, it's a felony). Once information has been transmitted, a player's judgment is affected. You cannot truthfully say, "I was always going to make that bid anyway," because you cannot *know* what you would have done. This claim is invalid even if you made your decision prior to partner's huddle, for two reasons: first, you may be unaware of how much the onset of the huddle crystallized the decision for you; second, and more important, *haven't you ever changed your mind*?

People sometimes come to me saying, "I have an ethical problem for you," and my answer is, "You've already ruined it." The situation should always be presented as a straightforward problem with no huddle. Even then, there is a major difficulty. Many errors occur because the player at the table says to himself, "It doesn't matter what I do." When a hand is presented as a problem, whether or not the responder suspects that it may be an ethical problem, he knows there is a relevant decision to be made, and this must affect his judgment. Strangely, this can work *against* players who are trying to justify a questionable call. Whenever I poll a hand where partner has made a penalty double, the expert almost invariably passes. His reasoning, conscious or otherwise, goes as follows: "He (the poller) probably doubled. I am not going to be the (only) one to pull the double and miss an 1100 penalty like his idiot partner did. If they can make it, I can always say I would never have doubled with that hand."

Thus a 'right' answer is assured. The same type of bias (in reverse) works itself on Directors and Committee members. The temptation to think, "I would never have let the opponents go +930 on this hand," is great. Of course, the good adjudicators are already aware of this tendency, whereas, I believe, the majority of players are unaware of the shift in their judgment when answering ethical problems.

Short Huddles

One of the most pervasive ethical problems that should be faced is the two-second huddle. It frequently conveys information to partner (intentionally or otherwise), and is extremely difficult to police. One of the most common examples is this:

OPENER	RESPONDER
1♣	1♠
2♠[1]	

1. After a short huddle

The short huddle shows three-card support.

A short huddle followed by a preference tends to show a double-ton, while a bid in tempo shows three.

In competitive auctions, the short huddle followed by a pass can be used as a weapon, either showing a desire to compete, for example:

WEST	NORTH	EAST	SOUTH
1♦	1♠	2♦	2♠
pass			

or showing doubt about the current contract, for example:

WEST	NORTH	EAST	SOUTH
1NT	dbl	2♣	dbl
pass			

Even if the existence of these minuscule huddles is conceded, it is unlikely that a favorable ruling could ever be obtained by the non-offenders. In most cases they won't even bother to call the Director.

Flexible Bids

An old bone of contention among experts revolves around the following question: is it better to explore carefully for the best contract by describing your hand, or is it better to take a quick stab at a final contract? The bashers believe that what they lose in science they more than recover in opponents' errors due to lack of information. The flexible bidders (or flexers) either do not agree with this, or feel more comfortable with the type of results they achieve.

It has been my experience that bashers are more successful than flexers, or at least more successful than I think they 'should' be. The major reason for this, I believe, is that bashers will be faithful to their style as long as partner is bidding in tempo, but after partner huddles, *bashers become flexers*. This means that when partner has a classic hand for his bidding the basher immediately bids the best contract giving away no unnecessary information, but when partner has a slightly flawed bid, the basher can check out alternatives by flexing.

For example, Ben the Basher holds:

♠ A 10 8 x x　♥ x x　♦ A Q x　♣ A Q x

and partner opens one club. Ben responds one spade and partner, after some consideration, rebids one notrump. Without the huddle Ben would have bid 3NT straight-away in order that the defenders might not be given any unnecessary information. However, after partner's informative huddle, Ben checks back with 2♣, reasonably enough, and partner bids 2♥. Recognizing the most likely meaning behind the huddle, Ben flexes with three clubs, natural and forcing. Partner bids three hearts, Ben bids 3NT. Partner bids four clubs, Ben bids four diamonds and partner bids six clubs.

Partner's hand was:

♠ Q　♥ A K x x　♦ K x x　♣ K J x x x

This was a well-bid hand, and if you believe a Committee could change this result you *may* be right; but there are countless hands such as this one where Ben will either gain or not lose.

Here is another situation:

OPENER	RESPONDER
1NT	2♥[1]
2♠	3NT

1. Transfer

Normally, this is merely a choice-of-games sequence, but responder may have a hand that only has slam possibilities if partner has at least three spades. Opener usually passes or bids 4♠ at this point, but he may also cuebid. Felix the flexer *will* cuebid, whenever he has a maximum hand, in light of his already having failed to pre-accept over 2♥. Of course, the disadvantage of the cuebid is that it may help the opponents' defense when partner, as expected, signs off. Therefore, Ben the Basher will only think of cuebidding when partner has huddled before bidding 3NT. It is true that an ethical partner would have planned his auction by thinking before he bid 2♥, but if Ben is alert it will come to the same result. Yet again, it's a case of 'heads I win, tails you lose' for Ben.

Flexers tend to remain faithful to their style and don't take advantage of partner's in-tempo bidding. They have no realistic recourse to the Director when the bashers flex. After all, they don't bash on *every* hand, just on the ones that look right to them — and who can rule on that?

FORCING BIDS

I once watched a world-famous expert at rubber bridge hold:

♠ 10 x x   ♥ K 10 x x x   ♦ x x x x   ♣ x

His partner, also an expert, opened 1♣. He responded one heart, and his partner jumped to two spades, whereupon he passed. As he left the table I whispered to him, "Do you know you were unethical on this hand?"

"What are you talking about?" he said. "Nobody huddled."

"Exactly my point," I replied. "What would you have done if partner had huddled before bidding 2♠?"

He thought about this and confessed that he would probably have rebid two notrump, hoping to hear 3♥, which he would raise to 4♥.

Obviously this doesn't feel right, but what can be done? If you call the Director after the hypothetical huddle example above, you might be told that a player has every right to bid after partner has forced. If you call the Director after the no-huddle example you might be laughed out of the building.

Even if the huddle came before the 1♣ opening, it would probably be 'right' to keep the bidding alive — partner might be 5-5 in the blacks with a near 2♣ opening and 4♠ might be cold. This case would be even more difficult to adjudicate.

FORCING PASSES

I remember reading about a case in which the Director was called after a huddle followed by a forcing pass. His ruling, in effect, was that the forcing pass conveyed a message of uncertainty and the huddle said the same thing. Therefore no unauthorized information was in existence. Since I don't wish to offend, I won't print my one-word reaction to this ruling. However, there seems to me to be a world of difference in this situation between an in-tempo pass ("I don't really want to do anything") and a huddle-pass ("I *really* want to do something").

A further problem can arise if partner, after the in-tempo pass, 'takes a view' and passes. No complaint can reasonably be made, even if the opponents admit that the pass is forcing, because no unauthorized information has been transmitted. The huddle-pass transforms the pass into a 100% forcing situation. Tough, huh?

DEFENSIVE CARDING

Some of the most egregious ethical improprieties occur during the play. However, the issues are so complicated, and sometimes so subtle, that often no one at the table realizes that anything untoward has happened. Let's look at a fairly simple situation:

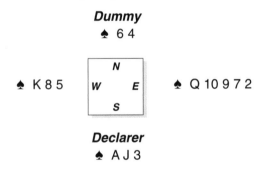

Dummy
♠ 6 4

♠ K 8 5

♠ Q 10 9 7 2

Declarer
♠ A J 3

East gains the lead in a notrump contract and shifts to the spade ten, on which everyone plays small. East continues with the spade seven, on which South, after some thought, plays the spade ace. West, after a long thought, unblocks the spade king East regains the lead, cashes the spade queen and the defense triumphs. But what if West had played that king smoothly? Perhaps East would have played him for a doubleton and tried an alternate defense.

Another position:

Dummy

♠ K Q J 6

You

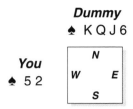

♠ 5 2

Declarer, who has opened 1NT, leads the spade three. You follow with the spade five, dummy plays the spade king, and partner mulls over the situation. What could be more natural now than for you, while partner considers, to plan your defense. Of course, you suddenly have no problem piecing together declarer's high cards. Indeed, after partner ducks, you may now even be able to make a fine play, such as ducking a king when declarer leads low from dummy to his queen in another suit.

Another example: you lead against three notrump and partner wins a later trick and starts thinking. Obviously, partner is not long in your suit — so... now you can quite possibly calculate declarer's distribution. (Incidentally, if partner returns your suit after huddling, it usually means he has a doubleton.) This sort of inference is a recurring ethical problem.

I found the following hand instructive:

Dummy

♠ J 5
♥ Q 7 3
♦ 7 4
♣ K Q J 8 5 4

♠ K 10 9
♥ A 8 5 4
♦ A 9 6 3
♣ 10 9

| N |
| W E |
| S |

NORTH	**SOUTH**
	1♦
3♣[1]	3NT
pass	

1. Invitational

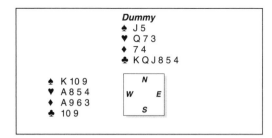

```
                    Dummy
                    ♠ J 5
                    ♥ Q 7 3
                    ♦ 7 4
                    ♣ K Q J 8 5 4
      ♠ K 10 9        ┌─────────┐
      ♥ A 8 5 4       │    N    │
      ♦ A 9 6 3       │ W     E │
      ♣ 10 9          │    S    │
                      └─────────┘
```

In a major matchpoint event, West, a world-famous expert, led the ♠10 to the ♠J, ♠Q, and ♠2. East returned the ♠4 — ♠3, ♠K, ♠5, and West continued with the ♠9 — ♦4, ♠6, ♠A.

Declarer led the ♣2 — ♣9, ♣K, ♣3 (upside-down signaling), then the ♦7 — ♦5, ♦K, ♦A. West now played the ♥A — ♥3, ♥10, ♥K, and paused for thought. Eventually deciding that either declarer had tried to steal a diamond trick or it made no difference, he returned a diamond. Declarer's hand was:

♠ A 7 3 2   ♥ K J   ♦ K Q J 10 8 2   ♣ 2

and he got out for down one (switch the ♥7 and ♥8 and he would have made it by squeezing East). Obviously, a club shift at trick seven would have set the contract two tricks; and this was clearly the correct defense — for two reasons. Firstly, if South had held the ♣A, he would have opened 1NT. Secondly, if declarer were trying to steal a trick, he would have attacked hearts, not diamonds, missing the queen.

What is my purpose in showing this hand? My point is that East ducked the club smoothly. Had he huddled before ducking, I have no doubt that West would have hit upon the winning defense. Had the declarer then claimed that he was damaged, he would have been told that this West did not require any extraneous help to get this obvious situation right. Further attempts to pursue the situation would probably have resulted in South being told not to make frivolous protests.

How many times have you heard a player on defense say, "I'm not thinking about this trick. I'm thinking about the whole hand." This normally means that the player does not wish to be caught thinking on some subsequent trick. Aside from the fact that this stratagem is a little disingenuous, there are several flaws to it. Firstly, information may be given to partner. Secondly, I've noticed that the player sometimes *is* actually thinking about this trick but doesn't want to admit it. Finally, in my opinion, declarer has a right to know on which trick you have a problem — I believe speedy thought should be rewarded.

Then, of course, there are the pairs who 'always think before playing to the first trick', except when they don't. Strangely enough, they usually forget to think when they want partner to continue with the 'obvious' defense. This brings us to the subject of signaling.

SIGNALS

When partner is winning a trick you often need to signal to tell him how to continue. Frequently, it is not clear which signal to give, so you play your card after deliberation. Now partner finds the winning defense and you congratulate each other after the hand. It feels very wrong to me that the tempo of the signal becomes part of the signaling method itself. I don't even want to mention (well, maybe I do) players who emphasize their clear-cut signals by huddling before making them — everyone knows *that's* wrong. But the case of the unclear signal may be just as bad, if not worse.

Take, for example, the Smith Echo. It may be really difficult to know quickly if you want partner to continue or switch. But, by thinking about this signal, you dramatically increase the probability of partner's knowing the winning defense. He will never go wrong when you have given him the 'winning' signal, and when you haven't he may be able to use bridge logic to figure it out. Meanwhile, had your signal been in tempo, partner was much more likely to have followed it blindly without thought.

Personally, I refuse to think before making a signal. I must admit this has cost me many tricks over the years, either because I made the wrong signal or because partner misread my ambiguous signal, or because he didn't even realize I was signaling. In fact, partner has sometimes tried to give me a ruff in the suit, which I doubt would have happened if I had considered my signal more carefully. For me, all this is counterbalanced by knowing that when my partner does the right thing, I feel completely clean about it.

SOLUTIONS

The first solution to some of the ethical problems I've cited is directed at the officials. It should be a matter of absolute routine for the Director to rule in favor of the non-offending side. The onus to appeal should always be on the huddlers. The only situation in which the Director should rule for the non-offending side is one where he feels certain that an appeal by the non-offenders would be frivolous. Also, it should be a grave decision for the appeals Committee to rule in favor of the offenders. Only in this way can a message be sent throughout the bridge world.

Completely solving the problem of short huddles is not practical, but there are certain things one can do to alleviate the problem. One is to take two to three seconds over *every* call, thus removing any inferences from fast actions. Another good idea is sometimes to plan your auction, huddling over the obvious action but preparing your next bid. If the timing of your huddles is somewhat random, it is difficult for partner to derive any advantage from them. The biggest crime in this area is to find yourself short-huddling when you want partner to bid, and fast-passing or fast-signing-off when you want him to pass. There is really no answer to the problem of flexible bids after huddles, except for each player to be guided by his own conscience. When partner bids quickly, consider allowing for the hands you 'know' he can't have. When he bids slowly, consider the advantages of being unscientific.

Regarding forcing bids, I believe every pair's convention card should state whether they are allowed to pass forcing bids. If the answer is 'no', then any violation would require extreme justification (i.e., if a player psyched an opening bid, he could pass the response). If the answer is (more commonly) 'yes', then bidding over a slow forcing bid would call for careful scrutiny. Similarly, every pair should have its forcing-pass agreements as clearly defined as possible on its card. Any situation not so defined could be deemed non-forcing by a Director or a Committee.

When partner huddles on defense, consider if it could be logical to play him for what he can't have. If so, you should play for just that. While partner is huddling (for example, thinking about ducking an ace), your only thoughts and plans, until partner actually plays his ace, should be made under the assumption that partner does *not* have the ace.

Thinking about which card to play on a future trick should be illegal, with two exceptions: being on lead, and the first trick. My suggestion for handling the tempo at trick one is as follows: the four players should jointly decide upon the length of time declarer should take before playing to the first trick (probably between ten and thirty seconds), with the highest number determining the tempo for that table. After tabling his hand, the dummy (or the opening leader) should wait for the agreed-upon period of time and then announce, "Play." Thereafter, any thought before playing a card must pertain to that card. Perhaps declarer should be allowed to play before the agreed time has elapsed if he wishes, but then the next player should have the right to play his card at any time up to the moment when dummy calls, "Play."

Thinking about a signal should be illegal. If your signaling methods frequently require you to huddle, perhaps they are too complicated.

Don't panic — nobody's going to go for this anyway. However, I am seriously suggesting that you try signaling only in normal tempo.

SUMMARY

Huddling is like ringing an alarm bell inside partner's head. It behooves us to attempt to overcompensate after partner's huddle in order to atone for all of the occasions of which we are unaware. If you never find yourself in the situation of making a bid or play which you 'know' to be the losing action, you cannot be an actively ethical player. Instead of attempting to rationalize your taking the winning action, try to justify the case for the losing action.

Why should you do these things when those around you do not?

Only because we must start somewhere, and the only person whose ethics you can truly improve is you, yourself. If we don't do this, we shall never be able to elevate this game which enthralls us to the level it deserves.

Re-reading the above a few years later, I was surprised to find that I still agreed with myself (unanimously). This was written when I was relatively green in these matters — I had yet to discuss them with other experts.

It is probably impossible for the game to be totally 'pure', no matter what rules are imposed or policies are followed. There will always be some players who will make a conscious effort to ensure that their tempo and demeanor reveal nothing to partner, while others would be quite happy if their partner made a winning decision based partially on a slight quickness or slowness or expression. Also, there will be some players who are careful that their opponents have all the information to which they are entitled, while others will need to be prompted with the right questions to reveal the same data.

I believe it is important to make it clear that a call for the Director, or an appeal to a Committee, is *not* an accusation. Some of the areas involved are very complicated, even for those well-versed in matters of ethical impropriety. Those who are inexperienced and do not 'know better' should never be made to feel that they have acted improperly or unethically. Each situation must be clearly and patiently explained — education without acrimony is the goal.

Many people are intent upon discouraging people from calling the Director and appealing to Committees. They feel that the game would be better with fewer such occurrences, and that the appellants should be considered as 'suspect' as their opponents.

I do not feel that it is important for the appellants to be regarded as suspects. This may be appropriate some time down the road, but for the moment every case is an education, and we need all the education we can get.

To make the total picture regarding ethics and the Laws more clear, the following are my comments on a few related subjects.

GUIDELINES FOR COMMITTEES

A) BREAKS IN TEMPO

One thing I look for when making a ruling on a huddle is this: was the (winning) action taken *as a result* of the huddle? Some other adjudicators seem more concerned with whether the action was *suggested* by the huddle.

At one of the Nationals, a player held something like

♠ Q 10 x x   ♥ x   ♦ x x   ♣ A J 9 x x x

and heard the bidding go (3♥)-3NT-(pass). The 3NT bid was made after a protracted huddle. This player leapt to 6♣, which was the winning action. Some experts felt that the 6♣ bid was neither suggested nor made more attractive by the huddle — it was just a ridiculous stab, and therefore should be allowed. I considered, based on the Committee report, that the huddle *induced* the 6♣ bid and, therefore, would have ruled that the player could not profit from it.

There was, and is, also the question of whether the opponents should get redress or keep their bad score (presuming it is possible to assign separate scores). Some believe that if, for example, 6♣ in the previous example was a 2% contract, then it is simply the 'rub of the green'. My philosophy, however, is that you should never do worse than you would have done against ethical opponents. So, whatever I take from A, I give to B (with an exception which I will discuss later). I believe both that this is equitable, and that it will create more general good feeling. Being unethical should be equivalent to taking a 0% play — like taking a finesse through a player who *can't* have that card.

In fact, if I believe that a player has taken an action with the intention of taking advantage of partner's break in tempo, I would rule against that player even if the action taken was contra-indicated. I believe that it is important to educate players to attempt to ignore breaks in tempo. On the other hand, if an action was taken with the intention of 'losing', and it happens to work, I would let that score stand. This might be a tough call — any doubt should be decided in favor of the non-offenders.

If there is no clear indication of what the break suggests, and I do not believe that the player was bidding (or passing) *because* of the tempo break, I would rule 'no penalty'. Obviously, the player's knowledge of the particular partner plays a large role here. After a while, in a regular partnership, you get to know what certain little things are most likely to mean.

I also believe, contrary to the majority, that one can rule differently for different standards of players. For example, the bidding goes (4♥)-*pass after break in tempo*-(pass). Now, there are some hands where I would allow an expert to double or bid 4♠ (if I feel that they would have done so anyway), whereas I would *not* allow a Flight B or Flight C player to bid if I feel that they would have been likely to pass out 4♥ but for the huddle.

On the other hand, there are many situations where an expert will be held to a higher standard and will 'lose'. My focus is always, "Did the break in tempo affect the result in this case?" I believe that we can only achieve justice by dealing with situations on a case-by-case basis. Everything else is a guideline.

Not all breaks in tempo are equal. Some huddles (or quick calls) are 'bad' — either because they describe one's hand to partner, or because they are likely to create a problem for partner. My current definition of a 'bad' huddle is one where partner is still 'involved' and:

a) The player breaking tempo has not promised any values prior to the hesitation, and now passes; *OR*

b) The player breaking tempo defines his or her hand by the tempo-break, i.e., minimum, maximum, extra length, slam interest, no slam interest, doubt when placing the final contract (frequently three notrump), lack of doubt when placing the final contract (also frequently three notrump), etc. *OR*

c) (Generally 'bad') The partnership is 'regular'. This means that each partner is more likely to be aware of personal predilections (for example, thinking before making an invitational bid — partner tends to have a bare invitation, or tends to have almost the values for game). Knowledge and experience of your partner can unfairly give you a clue as to which is more likely.

I feel that it is likely that there are other tempo-break situations which should be defined as 'bad'. I *know* that there are other *non*-tempo-break situations which should be so defined. For example, not correcting partner's mistaken explanation is a 'bad' infraction. Correcting at an inappropriate time is less 'bad'. The obvious solution is to have a list which Committee members can use for reference. Understanding which huddles are 'bad' and which are 'less bad' should help to create more uniformity in decisions.

B)   AVERAGING THE SCORE

In a knockout match, many Committees resolve what they believe are difficult issues by averaging the score. An example of this is as follows: the Committee determines that the final contract would have been four spades by a vulnerable North-South, but for some infraction. The four-spade contract depends upon a random two-way guess for a side queen. The Committee would take the IMP score for plus 620 and the IMP score for minus 100 and would average them.

While this seems fair on the surface, the problem is that rulings such as this spread into every other case, and suddenly every Committee decision becomes a Solomonic one. Even when there is obviously no damage, the procedural penalty is used to ensure that nobody (everybody) goes away happy (unhappy).

I do not approve of averaging the score. Instead, I prefer to settle upon one result, with all reasonable doubt being decided in favor of the non-offending side. While in certain cases this is extremely harsh on the side committing the infraction, it is necessary to send a consistent message to players, Directors and Committees. A consistently harsh approach by Committees should encourage players both to avoid breaks in tempo and to take no advantage of partner's tempo.

At most forms of scoring, other than knockout, it is possible to assign 'split' scores, i.e., give a different score to each pair. I generally disapprove of this practice since I feel that it is important that one does not receive a score inferior to that which one would, or might, have received against opponents who had not committed the infraction.

Once it is determined that the damage came as a result of the infraction, and was not simply subsequent to it, I would simply settle upon a single result, in favor of the non-offending side. The only case where I would feel that assigning split scores is justified would be one where the non-offending side has committed an egregious error (see next section).

C)   ANALYZING THE HAND

In analyzing what would have happened on a deal had there been no infraction, Committees should:

a) Assume that the non-offenders would have taken the winning view (especially when the infraction was flagrant);

b) Never assume that the offenders would have taken the winning view.

In analyzing what might have happened, I give the widest possible latitude to the non-offending side. To consider a mistake by the non-offending side egregious, the error has to be a total and unreasonable mind-loss *by that player's standards*. Even a 0% play by an expert may not be an egregious error — if the play appeared reasonable at the time. A revoke by any player is an egregious error.

Committees are far too likely to assign split scores based on subsequent 'errors' by the non-offenders. They fall into the trap of saying to themselves, "I would never have done that." The truth is that we all make mistakes, including big ones. The thing to remember is that the position was reached *only* because an opponent committed an infraction.

I would give somewhat less latitude to the non-offending side if the opponents' infraction was 'innocent', for example, a player giving misinformation as a result of having forgotten a partnership agreement.

D)   PROCEDURAL PENALTIES

Another policy I abhor is the 'procedural penalty'. I have two major objections: firstly, procedural penalties are inappropriate because bridge events should be scored based upon bridge results — either those which were achieved at the table or those which at least might have been achieved at the table; secondly, procedural penalties are not assessed uniformly.

When something 'goes wrong' at the table, but there is clearly no damage, then the Director is usually not called, and a procedural penalty is not even at issue. However, when there *might* have been damage from a similar infraction, and the Director *is* called, the case may or may not go to Committee. And a penalty may or may not ultimately be assessed by the Committee. Those pairs against whom no Director was called receive an unfair advantage. And even those cases which *do* go to committee are not handled uniformly. In fact, Committees have tended to assess procedural penalties almost randomly.

I believe that the current theory laid down by adherents of these penalties is that they should be awarded when, a) there has been an infraction but no damage, or b) there has been a flagrant violation of ethical or behavioral standards. Neither case is justification for a score adjustment. If the infraction was accidental or due to inexperience, and no damage occurred, there is no reason for a penalty. If, on the other hand, the violation was deliberate and serious, this should call for disciplinary action.

Now let's discuss some new ways to win IMPs. Firstly, always quiz your opponents to death — you might discover a failure to alert or you may elicit a mistaken explanation. For example, in a case from one of the Nationals a Committee gave half-an-IMP to East-West because South did not alert a gambling 3NT opening. I'll say it for the thousandth time. If there is damage, give redress. No damage, no penalty.

The other new IMP-winning strategy is to put your opponents' convention cards under a microscope. If they are not identical (or at least fraternal), you might be able to have your opponents charged with a one-quarter board penalty. This worked for a pair in the 1996 Nationals in

San Francisco (Case No. 18, which should have been deemed a frivolous appeal).

Until we get rid of these nonsensical procedural penalties, there will never be uniformity of rulings. In every case where a penalty is levied, a better solution exists.

The nature of the game is such that it must be partly self-policing, at least for the subtleties. For the rest, our best hope is the education of players as to their ethical obligations.

E) FLAGRANT FOUL

What *should* be done about blatant ethical improprieties? Currently, Committees tend to assign procedural penalties. A better method would involve a system of censuring offenders, and suspending them if they continue to abuse the game in this way.

F) FRIVOLOUS APPEALS

One policy which should become extinct is the $50 deposit for appeals at national and international events.* The policy is intended to deter appeals lacking merit, but it is obviously unfair, since $50 could be a substantial sum to some, but almost meaningless to others. Fining players for frivolous appeals by deducting matchpoints or victory points is unfair, for the same reasons that procedural penalties are unfair.

Generally, I do not believe that we want to deter people from appealing to a Committee. If the same player engages in repeated frivolous appeals, this should be a matter for disciplinary action.

---

*The ACBL did rescind the $50 deposit policy in 1997. They substituted a penalty point system which could lead to suspension for recurring appeals without merit. While this is an improvement, I feel that in our current state of confusion and disagreement over what is 'correct', few appeals have no merit.

Some people object to the way I blithely talk about the 'non-offenders'. They say that the complainers are suspects, just as much as those committing infractions. As I stated earlier, we haven't yet reached the stage where this should be considered. At the moment, we should welcome each appeal as an opportunity to further the education of the bridge community as regards ethical matters. Obviously, if the complaint has no merit, there is no need to award anything unjustifiable, nor indeed to adjust the score at all.

G)   APPEALS WRITE-UPS

Committee write-ups have greatly improved since the National Appeals Committee Decisions books have been published. These books are invaluable, and represent an irreplaceable summary of what is happening in the appeals process.

In breaks-of-tempo cases it is vital that the length of the hesitation be recorded. Of course, the protagonists often disagree, but even then, the information is useful.

The truth is that the Committee is in a much better position to make a ruling than someone hearing the 'facts' later. So let's arm Committees with guidelines and information in order to produce just decisions.

SCREENS

At the highest level of play, screens are normally used. This solves many of the ethical problems that arise, although a few minor new ones are created.

An example of a 'solved' problem occurs when partner makes an almost 'impossible' bid. For example, you raise 1NT to 2NT (natural) and partner rebids 3♣. If partner, without screens, had alerted your 2NT bid you would now be forced to pass. With screens, you can (if you believe there has been a misunderstanding) bid 3NT with no fear of reprisal. You are taking a risk, and have no unauthorized information.

Screen etiquette is important; if not adhered to, much of the good accomplished by the screen is nullified. Slapping bids down, talking, or even writing in a loud scratchy manner should all be *verboten*.

The player who bids first should have sole control of the tray. He can (and should) slow down the tempo, if he feels it appropriate to do so. The player who is second to bid should control tempo thus: he should pick out the bidding card he intends to use and show it to his screen-mate, but should not actually place it on the tray until he is ready to have it pushed under the screen. I suggest a ten-second limit for a 'screen huddle'.

ALERTING

The alert procedure seems to drive everyone nuts — with complete justification.

There are no good answers to some of the problems. Maybe it would be better to have no alerts — just automatic explanations of every bid. This would do away with the problem of a question by the non-alerting side giving unauthorized information to partner, but would give more unauthorized information to the partner of the player alerting than a simple 'Alert'.

For example, if you think that your bid shows a minimum, but partner thinks it shows a maximum, an 'Alert' will not help you evade a misunderstanding, but an explanation from partner may do so (unless you are ethical).

An amusing incident occurred when my teammates Bobby Levin and Peter Weichsel had the following auction:

Oppt.	Weichsel	Oppt.	Levin
WEST	NORTH	EAST	SOUTH
			1♦
pass	1♠	2♣	2♥
4♣	4♥	4♠	5♦
all pass			

Levin played his RHO for a lot of black cards, and lost some finesse to him. At the conclusion of play, the opponents informed him that 4♣ was Blackwood, and 4♠ showed two aces! Had he known this he would have made the hand. But the opponents were quite correct under the rules in force at that time, both in not alerting the Blackwood bid, and in not explaining it until no unauthorized information could be transmitted (i.e., after play had ceased). So North-South had no redress.

Perhaps there are no universal answers to the problems connected with the alert procedure but, at least at the top levels, the majority of them disappear (along with the ethical problems) with the use of screens.

SKIP-BID WARNINGS

Skip-bid warnings are a help in the area of tempo. The rules on how to use the 'Stop' card have frequently changed. I believe that the best method is this: the player making the skip-bid puts out the 'Stop' card and, slowly and silently, counts to ten. Then the card should be removed. The next player should study his cards until the

'Stop' card has been removed; then (one hopes) he should bid. If he uses more time then his partner has unauthorized information.

It is important to be consistent both in using skip-bid warnings and in pausing after them. Of course, when an opponent is 'never' going to bid it is less important — for example, in this auction:

WEST	NORTH	EAST	SOUTH
	1♠	pass	2♠
pass	4♠		

although I would still use it. There are many such instances where people think it irrelevant and, therefore, don't use it — or they ignore their opponent's use of the skip-bid warning and bid immediately. However, they are often quite wrong — the most common case being the simple 1NT-3NT auction. True, it rarely matters, but it is nice to have the option of considering a double (or a bid) without worrying about passing unauthorized information.

On the other hand, some auctions 'need' a skip-bid warning, even though they may not be skip-bids, for example:

WEST	NORTH	EAST	SOUTH
	1♠	dbl	pass
?			

The same applies to many other competitive auctions, especially those at high levels. And, I know that Zia believes a 'to play' redouble should be accompanied by a skip-bid warning.

The problem is in defining to which auctions this 'skip-bid warning' should apply. One solution could be a mandatory two-or-three-second pause before every call, but it is doubtful if such a requirement would be adhered to any more than the current skip-bid warning system is observed today.

Unauthorized information

The sort of unauthorized information gained from a failure to alert can often lead to what I call 'Jump-to-Game Syndrome'. JTGS occurs when a player fears that he and his partner are on different wavelengths.

For example, a player responds Drury (fit) and partner doesn't alert — it is amazing how frequently that player's next bid is a jump to four-of-partner's-major. And it is usually an unethical call. A player in this situation must bid as if partner had alerted 2♣; and it especially behooves him to make every effort to cooperate in a slam auction if opener's rebid over 'Drury' might have suggested a slam. For example, if opener 'raises' to 3♣ after Drury (having failed to alert), responder should 'raise' to 4♣ if he has four or more clubs. Opener may bid 5♣ at this point (whatever that means), bypassing four-of-the-major, or he may even cuebid (if his 'raise' to 3♣ was forcing). In either event it is likely that slam 'should' be reached by an ethical pair.

Misinformation ?

Some players give away *too much* information. The opponents are entitled to know your *agreements*. Agreements can be explicit or implicit, and they include partnership experience and knowledge of your specific partner. Agreements do not include what you *think* a bid means nor what you 'take' a bid to mean. Also, if you 'know' what partner's bid means, purely because of the hand you hold, you should not reveal this information. For example, you hold:

♠ K 10 8 7　♥ 10 9 x　♦ —　♣ J 10 8 x x x

LHO opens 2NT and partner bids 3♣. You are playing together for the first time, and your only discussion was "Landy." Obviously, your hand leads you to suspect majors. You should alert 3♣ (because you know something your opponents do not), but if asked you should say, "We agreed to play Landy, but we didn't specifically discuss it over 2NT." This is the same answer you should give if your hand were:

♠ Q J 10 x x x ♥ J 10 x x x ♦ x x ♣ —

and you had a sneaking suspicion that partner held clubs. This should hold true whether or not it appears to be advantageous to your side to give all the correct information.

There is great disagreement as to the appropriate course of action when partner misdescribes your agreement (either by commission or omission), but happens to describe your hand accurately . Many feel it is self-serving (and unethical) to correct partner in this type of situation. I strongly disagree

To give a comprehensive example, say that partner opens 1♦, playing a four-card major system, and you respond 1NT, which partner raises to 3NT. It so happens that your agreement is that you can respond 1NT with one or two four-card majors. Upon making the final pass, LHO asks partner, "Can your partner have a four-card major?" Partner, momentarily forgetting, answers, "No." Obviously, you should correct partner's explanation if you have a major.

But what should you do if you don't have one? Many would say nothing, thinking that it would be self-serving to correct partner. But, what if LHO now leads a spade, letting three notrump make when, had he been in possession of the correct information, he would have led a club and set the contract? Isn't it ridiculous that the opponents are doing worse because you (on the pretext of helping them) *and* your partner (by omission) misinformed them?

No, you should correct partner's explanation regardless of your hand. Your opponents are entitled to know your agreements and to make their decisions based upon that knowledge. You should simply say, "That's not our agreement — I can have one or two four-card majors." You should *not* need to add, "Although I'm not saying that I have one." That should be understood.

What happens when, in the above situation, LHO does *not* ask any question, as most would not? (This is why I used this example instead of the more normal situation — a 1NT response to 1♥, playing Flannery. In that case, many experts *would* think to ask whether responder could have a four-card spade suit.) Again, obviously, you should volunteer the information if you have a four-card major. And again, you should volunteer the correct information even if you *don't* have a major. This may seem slimy, but there is nothing slimy about it. As long as it is clear in everyone's mind that you should always give the opponents complete and accurate disclosure, there is no question of damage.

The reason that this issue has represented a problem is that so many people believe that, if an ethical opponent *volunteers* information, it must be describing his actual hand. The game needs to be rid of this notion. If it were universally accepted that you always give correct information *about your agreements*, this problem would vanish.

The third problem that could occur is: your agreement is that 1NT *does* deny a four-card major, but you surprisingly violated your agreement and you have one (or two). LHO asks, and your idiot partner says that you *can* have a major. Here, you should not correct partner's explanation. You were trying to deceive your opponents, but your partner got in the way. Tough luck.

One policy which is becoming more prevalent is for Directors to call players who have received misinformation away from the table and ask them if they would have taken some other action in different circumstances. I disapprove of doing this for two reasons. Firstly, it doesn't take a genius to realize that it is in his or her best interests to say, "Yes, I would, or might, have done something different." Secondly, and more importantly, the Director cannot put the player back into the exact position which would have existed without the infraction. Therefore, the player may not realize that he or she might have taken some different action. In other words, the player may not realize or understand that damage has occurred.

I think it is certainly okay to continue the practice of the Director asking a player at the table if they wish to change their last call. Opportunity can restore equity. In fact, maybe we could go one step further and back up the auction to the point of the misinformation. This could lead to the complication of unauthorized information from the infraction and everything subsequent to the transgression, but it might restore equity in some cases. At the very least, the idea deserves consideration.

SUMMARY

The following summarizes my suggestions for solutions to the problems I've raised in this last chapter.

PLAYER'S OBLIGATIONS

a) Never make "bullet" calls or plays. Try to keep an even tempo during the auction, and to show consistent interest in your cards.

b) Avoid, as much as possible, hesitating when your action will indicate the nature of your thought.

c) Use no mannerisms or gestures.

d) Describe your agreements as clearly and completely as possible.

e) Correct, immediately, any failure by *yourself* to give correct information, *unless* your discovery of such failure comes from unauthorized information from partner.

f) Correct any misinformation given by *partner* as soon as the hand is over (or the bidding is over and your side is declaring).

DIRECTOR'S OBLIGATIONS:

a) Rule in favor of the side that did not commit the infraction, unless you feel certain that an appeal by them would be frivolous.

b) Rule a legitimate score, not average plus and average minus. If in doubt, assign the maximum score that you believe the non-offenders might reasonably have achieved.

c) Do not necessarily trust a player's analysis — even if such analysis is against that player's own self-interest.

COMMITTEE'S OBLIGATIONS

a) Never 'decide' a case until you hear from both sides.

b) View self-serving statements with skepticism.

c) Determine all the facts, especially regarding the length of breaks in tempo.

d) Always rule a legitimate bridge score. Analyze the hand, giving the benefit of any doubt to the non-offenders, especially if the offense was 'bad'.

e) Explain your ruling clearly, completely and patiently to both sides. Be especially patient with the 'losing' side — do your best to ensure they understand the issues involved. Explain in an appropriate manner for their level of play.

f) In the case of a flagrant offense, make sure that the incident is properly recorded.

g) If there is a write-up of the Committee hearing, ensure that the report is clear, thorough and accurate.

CHAPTER EIGHT

WORLD CHAMPIONSHIP

Albuquerque, 1994

A massive entry — about 200 teams — competed for the 1994 Rosenblum trophy. My team was DEUTSCH (Kasle, Martel-Stansby, Bates-Rosenberg). Zia was not yet eligible to compete for the U.S., so I played with Roger Bates, and sometimes with Seymon Deutsch.

The round-robin did not go smoothly for us and, coming into the final day, we were all but eliminated. We needed to finish with three near blitzes (25 VPs) to have any chance. In the first match, against an Icelandic team, I played with Deutsch. We did well, other than the one hand where Seymon decided to make a wildly undisciplined bid (and that's being kind), in the hope that the opponents would do something even crazier. They didn't, and we went for 800 on a part-score deal. We won the match, but scored only 22 VPs. Seymon predicted that his crazy bid would cost us qualification for the knockout stage. Then he flew home to Laredo.

Bates and I played the last two matches with Chip Martel and Lew Stansby. We now needed two blitzes to have any chance — and we got them. This, along with some fortunate (for us) results in the other matches, allowed us to finish tied for fifth in our group. We won the tie-breaker for the fifth spot, but only four teams from each group were guaranteed qualification. A few fifth-place teams had a chance to qualify 'at large', and we were fortunate to be one of the ones who had a shot. But we ended up in a three-way tie for the last qualifying spot, and still had to compete in a playoff. Sometime during this prolonged tie-breaking, I called Seymon to tell him we were still alive and kicking. He made plans to return to Albuquerque.

We breezed through the playoff, and all the rounds of the knockout — until the final. It was difficult not to get caught up in the 'destiny syndrome', and to continue to play solid bridge; but Martel and Stansby were like rocks, playing throughout. Roger Bates was also in excellent form.

In the final, we played against a strong Polish quartet (Gawrys-Lasocki, Balicki-Zmudminski). The match was close throughout, but when it was over we had won the Rosenblum.

I would like to be able to report an interesting hand from the final, but I do not remember any that I feel are worth including in this book. Instead, here's a hand from the World Pairs which followed the Rosenblum that year.

I was playing with Hamman; we were leading the event going into the final session, and this deal was played in one of the later rounds. It was quite possibly the most incompetently declared hand in the history of the event (and maybe I shouldn't put any limits on it).

Hamman
- ♠ K 10
- ♥ A K x x
- ♦ x
- ♣ A K J x x x

Me
- ♠ Q J 9 7 5 3
- ♥ x
- ♦ A K 10 x x
- ♣ x

Beneficiary 1	Hamman	Beneficiary 2	Me
WEST	**NORTH**	**EAST**	**SOUTH**
			1♠
2♥	3♣	pass	3♦
pass	3♥	pass	3♠
pass	4♣	pass	4♦
pass	5♠	all pass	

Here is my list of excuses:

a) I was tired after playing the Rosenblum (not much of an excuse — everyone else competing in the pairs had also played in the Rosenblum, and I had had a session off every day).

b) I had to be up at 7 a.m. to play a 42-board session starting at about 8 a.m. (see parenthetical comment in (a), above).

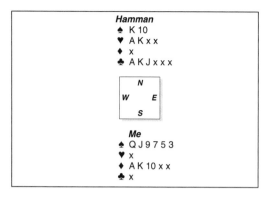

Hamman
♠ K 10
♥ A K x x
♦ x
♣ A K J x x x

Me
♠ Q J 9 7 5 3
♥ x
♦ A K 10 x x
♣ x

c) I am not a morning person and felt that being forced to play bridge before 11 a.m. was cruel, before 10 a.m. in-human, and before 9 a.m. grounds for a lawsuit.

d) I have an ulcer and caffeine is bad for me.

The auction leads to excuse (e); we had already missed a slam and a grand slam during the final session, and I was upset to see that we had missed yet another cold slam.

West led the club queen. I could see twelve tricks if the defense didn't make life too difficult, so I quickly won the club and called for the spade king. This held the trick, West playing the eight. What was that? A falsecard from ♠A8x? Not likely. More likely was that it was ♠A8 doubleton, since West must have the spade ace for his vulnerable overcall.

My play from here seemed irrelevant. In my soporific state I chose to play a diamond. I don't remember whether I was planning to cash the king or not (probably not), but I soon decided that the diamond play had been a mistake (the most accurate thought I had on the hand), and that I should play hearts first in case West had started with seven of them. When all followed to the ♥AK (I pitched a diamond), I had to play from dummy. A high club was safe if West had ♠A8 doubleton; but what if he had been false-carding? No, I'd better ruff a diamond and at least guarantee that I would make five. Since I had played that diamond earlier, I was forced to get off dummy with a heart. East pitched a diamond, but that wasn't too worrying. Since West had six hearts, at least one club and at least two spades, he could hardly have five diamonds.

So I 'cashed' the ♦AK of diamonds. East ruffed and played ace and another spade. Two down in 5♠. Not bad for a 'cold' slam. The full deal (as well as I can remember):

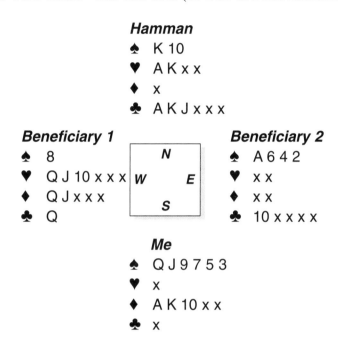

Hamman
♠ K 10
♥ A K x x
♦ x
♣ A K J x x x

Beneficiary 1
♠ 8
♥ Q J 10 x x x
♦ Q J x x x
♣ Q

Beneficiary 2
♠ A 6 4 2
♥ x x
♦ x x
♣ 10 x x x x

Me
♠ Q J 9 7 5 3
♥ x
♦ A K 10 x x
♣ x

I'm still not sure what is the best play at matchpoints. Perhaps ♥AK immediately, then ♦AK and ruff a diamond, playing on crossruff lines. However, on this layout I didn't need to find anything close to the best play to make twelve tricks. And I had made nine!

We finished second by a very narrow margin, thus avoiding my becoming the first player to win both the Rosenblum and the World Pairs in the same year.

If I had bid six spades (and made it) we would have won. If I had made twelve tricks in five spades, we would have won. If I had made eleven tricks in five spades we would have won.

Down one would not have been quite enough.

THE EPILOGUE

Sitting in a restaurant with Hamman after the event, I was brooding about my bridge shortcomings in general, and the 5♠ hand in particular. Then Bob asked me the fateful question:

"Did he save a low spade?"

For a second I didn't know what he was talking about. But I guess I must have woken up somewhat, because it suddenly hit me. Oh, no! I had done it again! Or rather — not done it again! If I had ruffed that heart with the *seven* of spades and East had carelessly ruffed the diamond with the *four*, I could underplay (and I'd certainly proved my ability to do that) the six and force East to concede the rest for down one. Going back further into the hand, once East 'erred' by playing the spade deuce, I could have always reached this position by retaining the three.

After having butchered the hand so badly, the opportunity was still there to do something really good.

And what about Hamman? After watching his partner murder the play and lose the event, he was still able to put his finger on a fascinating aspect of the hand. Not only a great player, but also a true 'student' of the game. If I ever grow up, I want to have his attitude.

A FINAL WORD

That's all I want to write about. There are many other things I might have added, and many other hands I might have included. Some of them didn't seem quite good enough, some of them I couldn't be bothered rewriting, and some of them I remembered too late. I doubt if I'll ever write another book, but maybe an article or three...